T0158558

– SUPER GREEN –
SIMPLE AND LEAN

First published in 2017

Copyright © Sally Obermeder and Maha Koraiem

All rights reserved. No part of this book may be reproduced or transmitted in
any form or by any means, electronic or mechanical, including photocopying,
recording or by any information storage and retrieval system, without prior
permission in writing from the publisher. The Australian *Copyright Act 1968*
(the Act) allows a maximum of one chapter or 10 per cent of this book,
whichever is the greater, to be photocopied by any educational institution
for its educational purposes provided that the educational institution
(or body that administers it) has given a remuneration notice to the
Copyright Agency (Australia) under the Act.

Allen & Unwin
83 Alexander Street
Crows Nest NSW 2065
Australia
Phone: (61 2) 8425 0100
Email: info@allenandunwin.com
Web: www.allenandunwin.com

Cataloguing-in-Publication details are available from
the National Library of Australia
www.trove.nla.gov.au
ISBN 978 1 76029 202 7

CUP AND TABLESPOON MEASURES: We have used
Australian cup measures, of 250 ml (9 fl oz). Please
note that the US and UK cup measures are slightly
smaller, approximately 235 ml (7¾ fl oz). We have
also used 20 ml (4 teaspoon) tablespoon measures.
If you are using a 15 ml (3 teaspoon) tablespoon,
add an extra teaspoon of the ingredient for each
tablespoon specified.

OVEN GUIDE: For fan-forced ovens, as a general
rule, set the oven temperature to 20°C (35°F) lower
than indicated in the recipe.

Recipe photographs: Ben Dearnley
Styling and props: Michelle Noerianto
Food preparation: Ross Dobson
Copy editor: Melody Lord
Nutritional analysis: Chrissy Freer
Index: Puddingburn Publishing Services
Design: Sarah Odgers
Set In 8.5/11 pt Gordita

Colour reproduction by Splitting Image Colour Studio Pty Ltd, Clayton, Victoria
Printed and bound in China by Hang Tai Printing Company Limited
10 9 8 7 6 5 4 3 2 1

— SUPER GREEN —
SIMPLE AND LEAN

140 SMOOTHIE, SALAD & BOWL RECIPES

SALLY OBERMEDER & MAHA KORAIEM

ALLEN&UNWIN
SYDNEY • MELBOURNE • AUCKLAND • LONDON

your guide to what's inside

WELCOME

If you had told us a few short years ago that green smoothies would change our lives (and yours), we might not have believed you.

Back then, Sally was in cancer recovery, needing to do something to help bring her body back to health after a year of intense chemo, radiation and surgeries.

Then came the discovery that drinking a blend of leafy greens, a heap of fresh veggies and a bit of frozen fruit was a game-changer. Who would have thought that it would make such a massive difference? Weight loss, improved digestion, growth (and regrowth) of her hair and nails. There's no doubt it helped Sal get her 'glow' back and gave her a tonne of energy. We soon discovered that it did the same for Maha: weight loss, better-quality sleep, softer skin and, like Sal, so much energy. We both felt lean and light and, well, just so good from the inside out.

While we were both fairly healthy, after we discovered the power of green smoothies we became a lot more conscious about clean eating for all our meals, and making sure we chose lean, whole foods as often as possible.

It's been very much a plant-based lifestyle, with added grains and lean proteins, boosted by extra sprinklings of superfoods and good fats and oils. We believe in eating well: delicious food that nourishes and satisfies. That's really what

has helped us both stay lean and energised. Plus we know we're getting a huge hit of vitamins and minerals each and every day. We're not super strict about it—we love our treats too—but we know we feel our best when we eat more fresh produce and unprocessed foods.

If you have followed our healthy lifestyle journey through our books, or on SWIISH.com, you'll know we believe in making life in the kitchen as easy and enjoyable as possible. There's no point in buying a million different ingredients, most of which you'll never use again, or following recipes that take hours of precious time. We want to share all we know about how to make healthy, tasty food in a way that's SUPER GREEN, SIMPLE and LEAN. Simple to prepare, simple to cook and filled with superfoods that make you look and feel super too! Everything in this book is what you have come to know and, we hope, love from us: food that's super-low in kilojoules (calories) and super-high on taste.

We've divided this book into four sections.

First up is *Smoothies*. Believe it or not, smoothies have come a long way since our first book, *Super Green Smoothies*.

We've discovered a whole raft of new superfoods and add-ons that will take your smoothie game to the next level and help you to feel better than ever! We've created, tested and devoured thousands of smoothies in the past few years. We hope you love all of these as much as we do!

Next up, *Salads*. We grew up in a house where Mum made us a salad every night to go with our dinner. We never went a night without it. These salad recipes are our hands-down favourites, but these days they're more than just sides—they're meals. They're super-lean and super-green and super-delicious.

Bowls **are the next big thing.** Trust us on this. Greens, grains, proteins and legumes, all decoratively arranged (definitely Instagram worthy) and full of nourishment. It's all about mixing and matching flavours and maximising nutrition. Bowls give you the best of everything, and we know you'll love them!

Here are some of our favourite *Snacks*: most raw, a few cooked and all a cinch to make. Whether you're having friends over, or keeping the family full between meals, these are great tasting and low cal. They include a whole heap of superfoods that you'll love and find yourself using more and more each day.

We truly believe that being healthy and cooking nutritious food can be a joy. As always, we hope you're inspired to live your best, healthiest life.

love Sally & Maha

the basics
& beyond

SUPER + SIMPLE TIPS

Who doesn't love a good shortcut? Don't get us wrong, we're all for making a meal from scratch, but in this day and age, we understand you can't always take the scenic route. That's why, if there's ever a way to cut down on prep time without compromising quality, we'll take it!

When it comes to staying lean, healthy and strong, it's the same story. While changing your whole lifestyle around is never going to be easy, there are ways to make things much simpler. You just need to know the right tips and tricks!

Here we've listed what we like to call 'Super + Simple' tips. These tips will not only save you time, energy and money but they'll also make getting on a healthy path a whole lot easier.

SIMPLE TIPS

* TAKE SHORTCUTS

Washing, chopping, grating and slicing can take up a lot of time. It's perfectly OK to take shortcuts! Buy prewashed and bagged baby spinach, other leafy greens and rainbow salads. Pick up precut carrot and celery sticks, and bags of fresh stir-fry veggies, which are available at most supermarkets. Use 40-second microwave rice or tinned beans, rather than cooking these things from scratch. When boiling eggs, we cook a few all at once and store them in the fridge for a few days.

* PRE-PORTION

When it comes to things you're going to be making fresh on a daily basis, it helps to pre-portion ingredients. For example, if you're going to be making a smoothie every day, try pre-portioning leafy greens into one or two cup portions to take the time out of measuring. Berries, broccoli and cauliflower can be separated into half-cup portions while larger fruits, such as avocado, lemons and limes, are best stored in quarters.

* IMPERFECT PRODUCE

When you're in the supermarket, fruit and vegetables that are in high demand or out of season can be super expensive. We recommend looking for the produce that may be slightly imperfect, as it is often a lot cheaper. Nowadays many supermarkets and fruit shops have a special section for these 'imperfect picks' and there's absolutely nothing wrong with these fruits and vegetables. They work especially well in smoothies, roasts and soups.

* BE PREPARED

Before you start preparing food, you should always make sure you have the right tools. The basic tools you should have are a blender, a food processor, a sharp knife, a grater and a peeler. It's also important to know the strength of your blender or food processer, as this will determine how much you need to pre-chop your ingredients. If you don't have a commercial-grade blender, you might have a hard time creating a smooth consistency (which some recipes may call for). In this case, simply chop tougher ingredients like broccoli into smaller pieces to make it easier for your blender to break them down.

* CHEAT THE SEASONS

It's always a shame if you can't get hold of your favourite fruits or vegetables because they're not in season. Don't worry though, there's always a way to get your hands on them. For example, we like to buy frozen mango from our local supermarket and keep it all year round. Frozen fruits and vegetables taste just as great and last longer, plus they still have all the nutrients you need. Tinned pineapple is OK when there is no fresh ripe pineapple available. Just make sure it's the kind that's in natural juice with no added sugar, and drain it of its juice before freezing.

* CLEAN AS YOU GO

This is a tip that we've learnt over the years and trust us, it makes a world of difference. If you've finished all your chopping, quickly wash and dry the chopping board before you start cooking. As soon as you're done with the pan, give it a rinse. If you clean little by little as you go, you'll be ready to eat as soon as you've finished cooking! You can sit down and enjoy your meal without having to worry about cleaning up later.

SUPER TIPS

* SATISFACTION IS KEY

Never finish a meal hungry. Yes, you should chew slowly to aid digestion, and yes, you should eat slowly to give your body a chance to see if it is full from what's on your plate. But if you finish a meal with room for more, you'll just end up reaching for snacks later. As our mum would always say, 'Finish your meal.' You need energy to work and play and, believe it or not, it's the best way to get lean and stay lean. At the same time, if your tummy tells you it's full, don't try to squeeze any more in.

* BE A HEAVY DRINKER

Drink plenty of water, at least 2 litres a day. If you're finding it tough, try infusing your water with mint, orange slices, cucumber, or strawberries and basil.

Drink at least 2 litres of water per day.

* MAXIMISE THE GREEN

There's a lot to be said for plant-based eating. Greens provide us with essential vitamins and nutrients plus long-lasting energy. When building your meal, aim to fill the majority of your plate with greens and vegetables. Then you can add carbohydrates and protein around this. This will ensure you're mainly eating low-kilojoule (-calorie), fibre-rich vegetables, while still getting all the essential nutrients you need.

* TAKE A SEAT

When we eat standing up or on the move, we often forget that we ate anything at all! We call this 'calorie amnesia'. When it's time for your next meal, make sure you plate up your food, sit down and enjoy every bite. After all, eating well is one of life's greatest joys.

* WATCH YOUR PORTIONS

One of the simplest ways to keep your weight under control is to watch your portion sizes. The recommended serving size for chicken is around 100 g (3½ oz), cooked. A typical serving of brown rice is about half a cup. This may not seem like a lot but the idea is to eat these things in moderation and then eat as many veggies as you need to fill you up.

* DON'T SKIP BREAKFAST

These days, a lot of people tend to skip breakfast because they're too busy. Everyone's trying to get out the door and get the kids to school or make it to the office on time. We get it! But breakfast is the most important meal of the day. It kickstarts your metabolism and stops you reaching for sugary snacks later on. Our Super Green Smoothies are the perfect option for breakfast as they take literally a couple of minutes to blend. Your body will thank you for it.

* DETOX YOUR PANTRY

If there are unhealthy snacks in the house, you will end up eating them! The best way to stay on track with a nutritious diet is to keep your pantry and fridge as clean as possible. Fill them up with nourishing snacks, including the ones in this book, so that your only option is to reach for something nutritious. This will help you to stay motivated and keep you on track.

* GET ENOUGH SLEEP   ZZZZzzᶻᶻᶻᶻ

Sleep deprivation can lead to weight gain. Getting enough ZZZs is critical for losing weight and it's also important for your body to have the recovery time from exercise. That's when your muscles repair themselves.

* BROWN BAG YOUR LUNCH

By making and packing your own lunch, you know exactly what you're eating and you'll be able to stay on track for your healthy goals. A great tip is to pull your lunch together while you're making dinner the night before. This recipe book is filled with recipes that you can make ahead and store in airtight containers to take with you to work.

A-Z SUPERFOODS

Ahhhhh superfoods ... once a term used solely within the walls of organic health-food shops. You can't go to your local cafe anymore without spotting kale or quinoa on the menu. And while we're still all about our chia puddings and crunchy kale salads, we've also been trying and testing out a whole heap of new superfoods too.

So what are superfoods?

Well, while there isn't currently any scientific definition, superfoods are any foods with very high levels of essential nutrients, vitamins and minerals. As a result, adding superfoods to your diet can have a world of health benefits. We're talking everything from soft skin, luscious locks and higher energy levels to reduced risk of disease. You can see now why they are called 'super' foods!

The latest unique, exciting superfoods have really brought the goods. Through-out this book, you'll find we use several of these superfoods to help give our smoothies, salads, snacks and bowls a super-powered punch.

In the meantime, here's an A-Z list of our favourites to give you the lowdown on what's what, what's hot and why.

✻ ACAI

Acai is a berry that originated deep in the Amazon jungle and may well be one of the most nutritious berries on earth. Acai is high in an antioxidant known as anthocyanin, which may help protect against high levels of cholesterol in the bloodstream and free-radical damage. On top of this, acai is also known as an immune booster, digestive aid and an energy booster; plus, it's super-delicious!

✻ AGAVE NECTAR

Agave nectar is a great natural alternative to sugar because it is not only tastier, it's a lot healthier too. Agave nectar is a liquid made from a cactus-like plant native to Mexico and South Africa. Its key health-promoting property is that it has a naturally low glycaemic index (GI), which means you get all that sweetness without the blood-sugar spike.

✻ ALFALFA

The alfalfa plant is rich in chlorophyll, calcium, magnesium, phosphorus,

potassium and just about every vitamin you can imagine. It's extremely alkaline, making it great for digestion. Noted for its detoxification properties, it can also help with fighting infection and losing weight.

* BANANA FLOUR

Wheat-free flours have become hugely popular in the last few years. While you've probably heard of almond and coconut flour, banana flour might be new to you. Made from green bananas, banana flour is gluten-free and has a delicious nutty flavour. It's also high in resistant starch, which helps with promoting good gut health. It works well when used in baking and salad dressings. Like coconut flour, banana flour tends to absorb liquid at a high rate, so you don't need to use much.

* BAOBAB FRUIT

This sweet, delicious fruit grows on the baobab tree in Africa but is usually sold in powdered form. The powder is made from the white fruit pulp, which is said to have marvellous nutritional and probiotic qualities. With a sweet, caramel, sherbet-like taste, it's the perfect addition to any nutritious dessert or snack.

The baobab fruit is grown on the baobab tree in Africa and usually sold in powdered form.

* BENTONITE CLAY

With the importance of gut health now firmly on our radar, keeping your insides clean is an absolute must. That's where bentonite clay comes in. It's traditionally used to promote internal cleansing and is slowly becoming a key part of many detox diets. It has also been claimed that it can help protect the immune system and fight off toxins.

* BLUEBERRIES

Blueberries are incredibly nutrient-dense berries. They're low in kilojoules (calories) and filled with vitamins, manganese and fibre. Flavanoids in blueberries also have the highest antioxidant capacity of all commonly consumed fruits and veggies, which helps to protect the body from free radicals that can cause cellular damage leading to ageing and diseases like cancer.

* BONE BROTH

Rich in protein and high in calcium, magnesium, phosphorus and potassium, bone broth is fantastic for your digestive system. One of the main reasons people drink bone broth is because of the collagen and gelatine, which help to repair your skin, hair and nails.

* CHIA SEEDS

An all-round superfood, chia seeds are definitely worth keeping in your pantry. They're high in calcium, magnesium, folate, iron, fibre and omega-3. They're also super-filling, and are a great addition to post-workout smoothies. Chia seeds can help to slow the ageing of skin by preventing inflammation and free-radical damage. Being high in dietary fibre, these seeds are also great for your digestive health.

* CHLOROPHYLL

Unlike most of the other foods in this list, chlorophyll isn't a fruit, seed or vegetable. It's the green pigment in leaves that helps plants to carry out photosynthesis. But that's not all it's good for. Chlorophyll is said to encourage healing in your body, promote cleansing, relieve swelling, help control body odour and even keep hunger cravings at bay. It's usually found in a liquid form, making it the perfect addition to your green smoothies or even water.

* COCONUT MILK

Not only is coconut milk delicious, it's also really good for you and can be used in many different ways. Unlike cow's milk, coconut milk is lactose-free so it's great for anyone with an intolerance (it's a favourite among vegans too). Rich and creamy, it makes the perfect base for milkshakes, smoothies, yoghurt and even ice cream! It's important to note that coconut milk does contain a high amount of fat compared with cow's milk. That's why we opt for coconut milks that are blended with rice or almond milk (available in cartons from the super-market)—still providing a delicious taste, but less fat for the body.

* COCONUT OIL

Extracted from the meat of a coconut, coconut oil not only helps to keep you feeling full but is also said to increase your energy expenditure so that you burn more fat. It does wonders for your skin and hair too.

* COCONUT WATER

This low-kilojoule, all-natural health drink is packed with electrolytes and minerals that fuel your body with essential nutrients and help keep you extra-hydrated. This beverage is a much better option than reaching for soft drinks, as well as being a fabulous addition to your smoothies.

* CUCUMBER

Yes, the humble cucumber … packed with water and fibre, it's essential for healthy digestion. It also contains anti-inflammatory flavanols, which may play an important role in improving brain health. This delicious green veggie is also high in antioxidants and B vitamins, which are known for helping to reduce stress. Cucumbers also contain polyphenols and phytonutrients that may help reduce the risk of certain cancers.

* DARK CHOCOLATE

Dark chocolate is packed with antioxidants that fight free radicals. It's also generally lower in sugar than white or milk chocolate. Try to choose dark chocolate that is 70–90 per cent cocoa to get the most benefits. Of course, as with any sweet treat, moderation is key.

EXTRA VIRGIN OLIVE OIL

Olive oil is very high in monounsaturated fats, which can help to lower your risk of heart disease. It also contains vitamins E and K and is loaded with antioxidants, which can help to fight free radicals and prevent oxidative damage.

FERMENTED FOODS

Fermented and cultured foods can be found in the form of pickles, kimchi, kefir and sauerkraut. Don't be fooled by the off-putting name: these foods can be seriously yummy! Plus, they make your belly happy. Fermented and cultured foods may promote the growth of beneficial bacteria in the gut, resulting in better digestion and a clearer elimination system. They can make you feel better, lighter, leaner, cleaner. Win!

FLAXSEED

Flaxseeds (also called linseeds) are the richest source of plant-based omega-3 fatty acids in the world. As a result, flaxseed is great for healthy skin, hair and nails. It also assists weight loss, overall digestive health and in lowering cholesterol. Flaxseed contains high levels of mucilage (plant gums) that can keep food in the stomach from emptying into the small intestine too quickly, thereby increasing nutrient absorption. High in both soluble and insoluble fibre, flaxseed may also assist with detoxification. We love sprinkling flaxseed meal on cereal and brekkie bowls or using it in baking.

GINGER

Ginger has strong antioxidant and anti-inflammatory effects. Ginger also appears to speed up the time it takes for the stomach to empty, thereby helping people with chronic indigestion and other stomach-related disorders. Research has shown that ginger may also help reduce cholesterol, lower blood sugars, and even help protect against Alzheimer's disease.

GOJI BERRIES

These nutritionally dense berries are native to the Himalayas. Although only relatively new to the Western world, they have been eaten in Tibet and China for thousands of years. With high levels of vitamin C, fibre and amino acids, goji berries also have the highest concentration of protein in any fruit. The best part, though? They taste amazing! We love using them in smoothies or sprinkled on salads and brekkie bowls.

HEMP SEEDS

Hemp seeds are the most nutritious seed in the world, some would argue. They are a complete protein source and filled with omega-3, -6, -9 and other essential fatty acids. We love sprinkling them on cereal or avo on toast.

INCA BERRIES (also known as Peruvian groundcherries)

Peruvian groundcherries, Inca berries, cape gooseberries or husk cherries are native to South America. These fruits are packed with vitamins C and A, iron, niacin and phosphorus. They're also high in fibre and have more protein than most other berries.

JICAMA

Jicama is a sweet and crunchy root vegetable with lots of health benefits! You can eat jicama raw, or cook and mash or bake it. Jicama root contains a prebiotic called inulin, which has a number of benefits that improve the bacteria in the gut. A real beauty-boosting food, jicama can improve the appearance of the skin due to the high quantity of vitamin C it contains, improving skin texture, speeding up the healing of any wounds and giving you an overall healthy glow.

KALE

Kale is one of the most nutrient-dense foods in the world. It is rich in vitamins A, K, C and B6, and minerals such as manganese, calcium, potassium, copper and magnesium. It also contains powerful antioxidants, including vitamin C and betacarotene, as well as various flavonoids and polyphenols. These flavonoids can help to lower blood pressure, reduce inflammation and protect against viruses and some cancers.

KEFIR

Basically, kefir is fermented milk made using kefir 'grains'. They're not really grains—they are a culture of yeast and bacteria—but they have a similar lumpy texture. Although it tastes a bit like yoghurt, kefir has about five times the probiotic nutrients. It also contains calcium, biotin, folate, magnesium and vitamins K2 and B12. What does that mean for you? Detoxification, a healthier immune system and stronger bones, fewer allergies and improved digestion. And it's delish. Add it to smoothies, oats or desserts, as you would yoghurt.

KELP

Kelp is a type of seaweed that contains high levels of iodine, which is critical for healthy thyroid gland function. It also contains vitamins C and E, which are both powerful antioxidants that promote blood-vessel health. On top of this, kelp contains calcium, boron and magnesium, which are important for maintaining strong bones and normal muscle function.

KOHLRABI

Also known as the 'turnip cabbage', kohlrabi is set to become a competitor with kale. This powerful vegetable is rich in vitamin C and helps to regulate fluids in the body. Eating enough of this can help to keep your skin soft, smooth and wrinkle-free, particularly around the eye area.

Kale is one of the most nutrient-dense foods in the world. Gotta love kale!

✳ KOMBU

Kombu is a delicious, salty seaweed that packs a serious nutritional punch. Unlike other seaweeds, kombu contains glutamic acid, which helps to add natural flavour to dishes. This acid also helps to break down the tough fibres in some foods, making them much easier to digest. Say hello to a happy tummy! It also has a high iodine content, which is essential for hormone production and normal thyroid function. On top of this, kombu contains lots of calcium and iron.

✳ LEMON

High in vitamin C, lemon also contains pectin, a soluble fibre that has been shown to be an effective aid in weight loss, particularly when combined with flaxseed. We love to use lemon juice in salad dressings or on its own in water.

✳ LUCUMA

Lucuma (pronounced loo-koo-ma) is definitely our new favourite when it comes to powdered fruity goodness. This lightweight raw powder is rich in antioxidants that may help to prevent disease and slow down the ageing process (*hasta la vista* wrinkles). It also contains protein and iron as well as complex carbohydrates for energy and brain function.

✳ MACA

Maca is a delicious, nutty-flavoured powder made from the root of the maca plant. It is high in free-form fatty acids, which help with hormonal balance, and also contains more than 20 amino acids. It is rich in magnesium, potassium, copper, zinc, manganese, phosphorus, selenium, sulphur and iron, and has more calcium than milk. The slightly sweet, malty flavour makes it a delicious addition to smoothies and desserts.

✳ MATCHA

It may look just like green dust, but there's more to it than meets the eye. Made of ground up green tea leaves, matcha is rich in antioxidants called polyphenols, which have been said to help with blood pressure reduction, blood sugar regulation, anti-ageing and even protection against cancer and heart disease. Not to mention, it gives your metabolism a major boost. Double win!

✳ MUSHROOMS (SHIITAKE)

Shiitake mushrooms contain all the essential amino acids along with an essential fatty acid called linoleic acid. Linoleic acid helps with bone and muscle growth as well as weight loss and digestion. In addition, this amazing superfood can also boost energy and brain function, promote healthy skin and support the function of the immune system.

✳ NUTS

Full of protein and heart-healthy fats, nuts are fantastic for your health. They also contain vitamin E, which is amazing for your skin and hair. We like to eat them as a snack or in the form of nut butter;

just make sure you get the kind that isn't loaded with sugar and other additives.

* OAT MILK

If you're lactose-intolerant, vegan or simply want to avoid dairy, then this one's for you! A nutritious alternative to cow's milk, oat milk is made from whole oats and contains 10 essential minerals and 15 vitamins. A single glass of oat milk can contain up to 35 per cent of the recommended daily allowance of calcium. It's also lower in fat than normal milk.

* PAPAYA

Papaya is a very nutritious tropical fruit full of antioxidants that can help reduce inflammation, fight disease and keep you looking young. Studies have shown that these antioxidants are more easily absorbed by the body than those in many other fruits.

* QUINOA

This grain-like seed has rocked the health-food world, and for good reason! Not only does it contain good stuff such as essential fatty acids, proteins, anti-oxidants and heart-healthy fats, its grain-like consistency makes it a super-nutritious alternative to dinner-time staples such as pasta and rice. It is rich in protein, which leaves you feeling fuller for longer.

* RAW CACAO

Unlike the cocoa in most chocolate, raw cacao is made by cold-pressing unroasted cocoa beans. This removes the fat from the beans and keeps all the living enzymes intact. Raw cacao is an amazing antioxidant that can help to repair the damage caused by free radicals and may even reduce the risk of cardiovascular disease and cancer. In fact, there are so many antioxidants in raw cacao that they make up 10 per cent of its weight. With the addition of oil and/or sweetener, cacao has a very chocolatey taste, making it perfect for both smoothies and desserts!

* SACHA INCHI SEEDS

This crunchy, nutty-flavoured seed is a traditional Incan snack that grows in the Peruvian rainforest. Roast them and sprinkle them over salads and yoghurt, or simply eat them all on their own! Rich in omega-3 acids and protein, they make the perfect guilt-free snack.

* SPINACH

Spinach is a very good source of vitamin K, which is important for maintaining bone health. It is high in antioxidants, including vitamins C, E and A as well as manganese, zinc and selenium, all of which lower the risk of health problems related to oxidative stress. The phytonutrients in spinach may also have anti-inflammatory and cancer-preventing benefits.

✳ SPIRULINA

Spirulina is a blue-green algae that is sold in liquid form. Containing protein, vitamin B1, vitamin B2, vitamin B3, copper, iron, magnesium, potassium and manganese, it's one of the most nutrient-dense foods on the planet. It also offers high levels of antioxidants, which can reduce damage to our cells, thereby also reducing chronic inflammation in the body. Research shows that spirulina may also help reduce blood pressure and control blood-sugar levels.

✳ TURMERIC

This orange spice has amazing antioxidant and anti-inflammatory benefits. As a result turmeric may be very helpful in protecting against illnesses in which chronic inflammation plays a role.

✳ UMEBOSHI (fermented Japanese plum)

Known for its incredible alkalising effects, umeboshi is slowly growing in popularity. It can help to stimulate digestion, eliminate toxins from the body and reduce fatigue. It can also boost your immune system and help to keep colds away.

✳ VINEGAR (apple cider)

Apple cider vinegar promotes healthy digestion, cellular cleansing and the growth of good bacteria. It is also said to help promote weight loss and can be used on the skin to relieve acne and as a shampoo to make your hair shine.

✳ WHEAT GRASS

Wheat grass contains a special enzyme that helps slow down the ageing process. Rich in protein and essential vitamins, and containing many essential minerals, wheat grass is considered to be a nutritionally complete food. We love using it in smoothies or grinding it up and taking it as a shot!

✳ XIGUA

This is the Chinese name for watermelon. Watermelons are mostly made of water, which makes them very low in kilojoules (calories) and also hydrating. They're also rich in vitamins A, B6 and C, as well as lycopene and lots of antioxidants and amino acids.

Hey! We needed an 'X' superfood!

✳ YOGHURT

Yoghurt is one of the best sources of calcium you can get. It also contains probiotics, which can help to boost your immune system and encourage good bacteria in the gut. Choose one without added sugar or flavouring.

✳ ZUCCHINI

Zucchini (courgette) is a delicious, low-kilojoule (-calorie) green vegetable that can be used in many different ways. It is a great source of vitamin C and potassium, as well as folate, which is super-important during pregnancy.

GET READY

In case you hadn't realised by now, we're all about our veggies and fruits. Whether they're fresh or frozen, you can guarantee they'll find a way into our meals.

Over the years, we've developed a pretty good idea about what sorts of fruit and veggies we need on hand. While some can be purchased fresh all year round, others might need to be bought seasonally and then frozen. Either way, they are nutritious and, if you prepare them properly, they'll always be delicious.

In recent years, there's been more and more emphasis on sustainability, especially when it comes to food choices. We love to use whole vegetables and fruits, rather than throwing away the peel, seeds, stems and roots.

Here we've listed some of the items that we consider our fridge and freezer staples. Whether you're whipping up a smoothie, a healthy snack or a nourishing bowl, you'll want to have these items on hand ...

Avocados are full of healthy fats which are great for hair and skin.

FRIDGE + FREEZER

✳ AVOCADOS

Adding a bit of avo is always worth it, even if it does set you back a few extra dollars. Aside from being totally delicious, this creamy fruit is full of healthy fats, which are great for your hair, skin and nails. We love eating them with eggs, in salads or as a more nutritious alternative to butter.

✳ BABY GREENS

What started off as a baby spinach obsession has led us to start using all sorts of 'baby' leaves. These days, it's easier to find baby kale, baby rocket (arugula), baby bok choy and so many others at your local green grocer or supermarket. Baby vegetables tend to be a lot sweeter than their larger siblings, which makes them a great option for smoothies. Baby greens are also full of all the vitamins and minerals you need to increase vitality and restore energy. We love to keep some fresh and some frozen.

* BANANAS

Sweet, delicious and totally satisfying, bananas are the ultimate energy food. Wrapped in their own natural packaging, they're also a quick and easy snack to have on the go. Bananas are rich in potassium, an essential mineral for maintaining healthy blood pressure and heart function. Don't keep your bananas in the fridge though (they'll go brown!). Instead keep some in a fruit bowl and others chopped up in bags in the freezer to use for smoothies and as an alternative to ice cream.

* BERRIES

We eat berries pretty much every day. It's a good idea to keep some in the fridge and some frozen. Fresh ones can be used as a topping on a brekkie bowl, while frozen ones are perfect for smoothies or a snack. Berries are rich in antioxidants, so eat up!

* BROCCOLI

When you think of all the most nutritious veggies, broccoli is probably the first thing that comes to mind. Broccoli is super-versatile and can be used in salads, stir-fries and smoothies, so it's always good to have on hand. With dietary fibre, minerals and vitamins A, B and E, it's the perfect way to supercharge any meal. We like to keep a little in the fridge and a little in the freezer.

* BRUSSELS SPROUTS

Isn't it funny how the food you hated as a kid can become one of your ultimate faves? You just need a few fabulous recipes to learn how to maximise its flavour. We love Brussels sprouts in salads or cooked as a side dish. With huge amounts of antioxidants, fibre, folate and vitamin C, Brussels sprouts are amazing for your health. We like to keep some in the fridge in case we're in need of an easy side dish.

* CAULIFLOWER

Cauliflower is one of those ultra-versatile veggies that can be turned into just about anything you like. We're using it to make smoothies, as a rice substitute and even to make bread and pizza bases. On top of being low in kilojoules (calories) and carbs, cauliflower is also full of nutrients such as omega-3 fatty acids, choline, fibre, manganese, biotin and phosphorus. Always keep cauliflower in your fridge so it maintains its freshness.

* CHEESE

A little bit of feta goes a long way! Goat's cheese is also a winner thanks to its creamy texture and mild flavour. Haloumi is a must-have too. (Can you tell we love our cheeses?) These cheeses work with salads, zucchini noodles, eggs, in toasties and just on their own.

* COCONUT WATER

We like to keep coconut water handy to use in smoothies or even just to drink on its own. Coconut water is rich in electrolytes, which makes it ultra-hydrating. Look for a version that contains no added sugar.

* EGGS

Packed full of vitamins, minerals, high-quality proteins and good fats, eggs are like little nutrition powerhouses. An egg is also the one ingredient that seems to turn up in breakfast, lunch, dinner and dessert! So it's a good idea to always have some handy.

* FERMENTED FOODS

If you have poor digestion, fermented and cultured foods are going to be your new best friend (see our section on gut health, page 46). They promote the growth of healthy bacteria in the gut, which results in better digestion and a cleaner elimination system. You can find these foods in the form of pickles, kimchi, kefir, kombucha and sauerkraut. You'll see we use some of these in recipes in this book.

* FRESH HERBS

Herbs are a must-have for any kitchen. They're perfect for adding a tonne of flavour to meals. We like to keep ours in the fridge, but keeping some in the freezer will help them last longer. Try chopping some up and freezing them in an ice-cube tray with a little water or oil. They're perfect to throw into the pot when you're making curries, sauces or soups.

* GRAPEFRUIT

Probably one of the most underused fruits, grapefruit has recently had a resurgence in popularity. The unique, bitter–sour taste makes it a delicious addition to salads and smoothies. Both pink and red grapefruit contain the anti-oxidant lycopene, which helps to fight free radicals that can damage your cells. Grapefruit is also quite low in sugar and kilojoules (calories) compared to some other fruits.

* KALE

Kale has fast become one of the most popular greens you can buy. It is slightly more nutrient-dense than spinach but also a bit tougher. If we're using it in a salad, we like to massage it with a bit of olive or coconut oil first. This will help to soften the leaves a bit and make it easier to eat. See page 19 for more information.

* KOMBUCHA

Kombucha is a fermented tea-based drink that is made using SCOBY (symbiotic culture of bacteria and yeast). It may not sound very appealing, but it's actually delicious! This healthy, probiotic beverage is usually sweet and sparkling. It's a yummy alternative to soft drinks.

* MEDJOOL DATES

Medjool dates are our choice because they're super sweet and soft. They're also very high in fibre, which helps you feel full for longer. You can use dates in brekkie bowls, smoothies, desserts and even to make a substitute for caramel! They hit the spot and are the perfect snack to keep in your fridge.

✳ NON-DAIRY MILK

Plant-based milk isn't just for vegans and the lactose intolerant. Soy milk is high in protein, and almond milk is low in kilojoules (calories). These are all great alternatives to use in smoothies or in cooking. Hazelnut milk is full of vitamin B, and coconut milk is rich in vitamins, minerals and fibre; both are great as a substitute for thin (pouring) cream due to their similar consistency. Be sure to read the labels, though, and choose one without added sugars and flavours.

✳ POMEGRANATE SEEDS

A few years ago, pomegranates weren't a hugely popular fruit. Now, the seeds are finding their way into all sorts of different dishes. Known for their antioxidant and antiviral properties, pomegranate seeds are amazing for your health. We love to keep them on hand to throw in smoothies or to garnish salads or brekkie bowls. We even eat them all on their own!

✳ RED CABBAGE

We're always looking for ways to introduce more colour into our diet, which is why red cabbage has become a staple in our fridge. It works well mixed in with leafy greens as a salad base, as well as in stir-fries and sandwiches. Another great thing about cabbage is that when it's too old to be eaten fresh, you can chop it up and ferment it in a jar. You can then keep it for weeks!

✳ TAHINI

This one's not as commonly used as it should be. Tahini is an oily paste made from finely ground sesame seeds. It's full of vitamins and is a richer source of protein than milk, sunflower seeds, soya beans and most nuts. It's great for making your own hummus, drizzled on a salad, or even on toast!

✳ YOGHURT

One thing we always have in our fridge is a tub of good-quality yoghurt. It's perfect for breakfast, as a snack, or even as a substitute for cream in a dessert. Not to mention, it's seriously good for you too! Yoghurt can be full of live, active cultures that help to balance the microflora in your intestines and keep your tummy happy.

With organisation comes empowerment.

PANTRY

If you want to live a healthy lifestyle, prepping your pantry is key. Keeping your cupboards full of clean, nutrition-rich ingredients will not only prevent you from eating unhealthy snacks but it'll also help to keep you motivated.

Over the years, the list of items that we would consider pantry essentials has definitely expanded. With new knowledge emerging about what's nutritious and what's not, people are beginning to question whether some staples still belong in their pantry. What were once considered rare and hard-to-find superfoods have now been given their own section in the supermarket. Many sugars are being replaced with natural sweeteners and fat (good fat) is once again our friend. As a result, most pantries are in need of an update.

While we use hundreds of different ingredients throughout this recipe book, you'll find there are a few that will pop up over and over again. To make things easier for you, we've put together a list of all the items that we consider our pantry staples.

✳ ALMOND MEAL

Almond meal is a fantastic, low-carb alternative to real flour because it's high in protein and good fats but free of gluten. You can either buy it from the supermarket or make your own by processing almonds to a powder and storing it in an airtight container in the fridge.

Make your own—it's super easy.

✳ APPLE CIDER VINEGAR

This tangy liquid is a definite must-have for your pantry. Not only does it make a great addition to marinades, dressings and sauces, it's amazing for your health too. Apple cider vinegar can help to regulate blood sugar, delay the effects of ageing and promote weight loss. It's important to check with your doctor if you have diabetes or insulin sensitivity, but for otherwise healthy people we recommend drinking a teaspoon or two mixed with a glass of water every morning.

✳ BLACK RICE

Black rice has been eaten in regions of Asia for thousands of years but today this type of rice is gaining popularity elsewhere as people discover all the amazing health benefits it has to offer. Now you can find it in sushi trains, restaurants and health-food stores all over the world. Of all the rice types, black rice is the richest in powerful disease-fighting antioxidants.

It's also loaded with fibre and may help prevent weight gain. We love to keep it on hand to cook as a nutritious side dish or to use in poke bowls.

✳ BROWN RICE

We like to substitute brown rice for white rice when we can. It has a lovely chewy texture that just seems to go well with everything! It's also high in complex carbohydrates and full of hunger-busting fibre.

✳ BUCKWHEAT

Surprisingly, buckwheat has nothing to do with wheat: it's actually a nourishing seed so it's perfect for anyone who needs a gluten-free diet. It is full of vitamins, minerals and nutrients as well as fibre. We use it to give smoothies a thick, creamy texture, which is perfect for creating layered smoothies.

✳ BUCKWHEAT NOODLES

Buckwheat or soba noodles are a great alternative to regular noodles due to the fact that they have a low glycaemic index (meaning the body uses the energy more slowly). You can even buy gluten-free noodles. They're also super-easy to cook! You just pop them in a bowl of hot water for a few minutes, strain them and they're done! You can then toss them through salads, add them to stir-fries or eat them just as you would regular noodles.

✳ CACAO POWDER

Most people who like to bake have a box of cocoa in their cupboard, but if you want to up the nutritional value then try cacao powder instead. It's perfect for adding that yummy, chocolatey taste to smoothies, snacks and desserts.

✳ CHIA SEEDS

We've already mentioned the amazing health benefits of these little seeds (see page 15), so they had to make it onto our essentials list. You can use them in many different breakfast, dessert and snack recipes, or sprinkle them over salads.

✳ COCONUT FLOUR

With the growing emphasis on sustainability, coconuts are now being used for all their worth. Not one ounce of flesh goes to waste! Made from ground and dried coconut meat, coconut flour is fast becoming a modern pantry staple. High in fibre, rich in protein and 'good' fats, gluten-free and low in carbohydrates, it's one of the most nutritious flours you can use. While it appears quite light and airy, coconut flour can be very dense when cooked. For this reason, it works well in baked goods such as muffins, cakes and bread.

✳ COCONUT OIL

Coconut oil is our favourite alternative to regular oil, and for good reason! It's rich in essential fatty acids, it's great for your hair and skin, and it can be used in just about any recipe. It also tastes great!

✳ COCONUT SUGAR

Coconut sugar is one of the most nutritious sugars you can eat. It's also one of the most sustainable sugars in the world. We love it because it has an extremely low GI compared to refined cane sugar. It also works in a similar way to brown sugar in that it caramelises and creates a beautiful, rich flavour.

✳ FLAXSEED MEAL

Like almond meal, flaxseed meal is a great filler for foods like bread, cakes and cookies. It's an amazing source of minerals, fibre and omega-3 fatty acids. To get the most out of flaxseeds, you need to grind them up. That's why flaxseed meal is so great!

✳ HERBS AND SPICES

Put simply, herbs and spices are the key to adding maximum flavour to any dish. Not to mention, most of them are quite high in antioxidants, and the hotter kinds of spices in particular can help speed up your metabolism. Cinnamon and nutmeg are our favourites when it comes to making sweeter dishes, while turmeric, coriander, cumin, rosemary and basil are great for curries and soups!

✳ MONK FRUIT SWEETENER

Sold under the brand name Norbu, this natural sweetener has 96 per cent fewer kilojoules (calories) than refined cane sugar. Like stevia, it doesn't impact on insulin or blood-sugar levels.

✳ NUTS

Nuts are full of 'good' fats that help you feel full, making them the perfect snack to keep in your pantry. Almonds are our favourite because they're one of the lower kilojoule (calorie) options, and they taste delicious when roasted and sprinkled with a bit of tamarind and sea salt.

✳ NUT BUTTER

Most people will have a jar of peanut butter in their pantry but we prefer to use all natural almond, cashew or hazelnut butter instead. Not only are nut butters packed full of 'good' fats and protein but you can use them in just about everything—smoothies, sauces, baking, for balls or spread on toast. Personally, our favourite way to eat nut butter is by smearing it all over a banana or an apple. Trust us, it's amazing.

✳ OATS

Oats can be used in many different ways. Cook them for breakfast, add them to smoothies to keep you full for longer, use them to make biscuits (cookies), or even grind them into flour! They're rich in complex carbohydrates and taste absolutely delicious.

* QUINOA

This grain-like seed is a must-have for any pantry. It's the perfect high-protein, gluten-free alternative to the usual pasta and rice. Believe it or not, you can even use it to make porridge! It tastes delicious.

* RICE MALT SYRUP

This is one that pops up in a lot of our recipes. That's because it's probably the most nutritious sugar-swap you can get. Made from 100 per cent organic brown rice, this sweet syrup is high in complex carbohydrates and completely fructose-free. It's fantastic for making snacks, or adding to salad dressings in place of refined cane sugar or brown sugar.

* STEVIA

If you're trying to cut down on sugar in your diet, you have to keep some of this sweetener in the house (or in your handbag for coffee on the go). Stevia is an all-natural, zero-kilojoule (-calorie) substitute for sugar. It's also a lot sweeter than granulated sugar, so you don't have to use as much.

* SUPERFOOD POWDER

These days, having a green superfood powder in your pantry is the norm. There are lots of brands on the market but we like to add our own, which we created. We use SWIISH DELIISH Super Green Superfood Powder in smoothies, sprinkle it on yoghurt, add it to our snack balls, or even just mix it in with a bottle of water and drink it on the go. Keeping superfood powder in plain sight in your pantry will make you more likely to use it, which is why it's made our pantry essentials list. We'll show you how to use it in balls (page 230) and pops (page 243). You can pick it up from shop.swiish.com.

* VANILLA EXTRACT

As the importance of sticking to natural foods becomes better known, vanilla extract is slowly taking the place of vanilla essence. While many types of vanilla essence are imitations that contain chemically manufactured flavouring, vanilla extract is a natural product derived from vanilla beans. With a syrupy texture and a sweet taste, we love using vanilla extract in smoothies, breakfast dishes, healthy snacks and desserts.

FRUITS WE LOVE AND GREENS WE SWEAR BY

Everybody knows that when it comes to keeping healthy and energised, lots of veggies and fresh fruit are your friend!

Packed with just about every vitamin and mineral you can think of, veggies and fruit have a world of health benefits that non-plant-based foods just can't beat.

Over the last couple of years, there's been a whole lot of new research about the dangers of low-fat fad diets and misleading labels. As for sugar, that has become one of the hottest topics on the health scene. The so-called 'sweet poison' has been pinned as a major culprit when it comes to modern-day health problems.

The issue is that too many people are putting fruit in that category and thinking that fruit—one of the most nutritious, vitamin-rich foods we can eat—is part of this new category of things we shouldn't eat. We really do not believe this is the case. While refined, processed sugars or sugars consumed in concentrated amounts are certainly not great for your health, low amounts of natural sugar (such as the kind of sugar found in fruit) are absolutely fine. In addition, when you consume fruit, you are also consuming fibre, minerals, vitamins and antioxidants, which are essential for maintaining good health.

Over the years, we've managed to get a pretty good idea of what certain fruits can do for our health. Berries, for example, are extremely high in antioxidants, which can do wonders for your skin. Bananas, on the other hand, are a great source of starchy carbohydrates and can provide the ultimate energy boost. Citrus fruits such as oranges and lemons provide vitamins that can help fight off colds and flu. We could go on for hours!

In terms of vegetables, each type has its own unique set of health benefits. Typically, most vegetables are rich in vitamins such as C, K, E and A. Most are also high in fibre, low in sugar and fat-free. This is precisely why piling your plate high with a medley of veggies will ensure you get maximum nutritional benefits without causing a kilojoule (calorie) overload. Of course, this will also depend on what type of veggies you're eating.

While we're big believers in the idea that every veggie should make its way onto your plate at some point (eat the rainbow!), there are a few we swear by. For the most part, these include dark

Amazingly, watercress has more vitamin C than oranges and more calcium than milk.

green leafy vegetables such as **spinach**, **kale** and **silverbeet** (Swiss chard). The reason for this is that these types of vegetables typically provide more nutrients than most other foods. Plus, they're just super easy to cook with! You can toss them into salads, throw them in a stir-fry, bake them into a frittata or even blend them in a smoothie.

Aside from your basic salad-style leaves, there are lots of other vegetables that are also classified as leafy greens.

Watercress, for example, is a leafy green that tends to be underused. With more vitamin C than oranges, more calcium than milk and more iron than spinach, it's great for switching up our salads so we work some watercress in on a regular basis.

Cabbage is also a favourite of ours. An excellent source of vitamin K, vitamin C, selenium, iron and manganese, cabbage is probably one of the most nutritious (and tastiest!) ways to add crunch to your salad.

Brussels sprouts are another member of the leafy green family. If you're thinking, 'ewwww, Brussels sprouts', we promise that you'll find some incredibly delicious ways (yes, delicious!) to enjoy them (yes, enjoy!) in this book. Not only do Brussels sprouts taste great but they also contain huge amounts of antioxidants, fibre, folate

and vitamin C. There are so many options here to choose from!

Then of course, there's **broccoli**. How could we forget broccoli? Packed full of fibre and antioxidants, broccoli is considered one of the healthiest leafy greens in the world. One thing that you may not know about broccoli is that while the florets are amazing for your health, the leaves of broccoli may be even better! Recently deemed a new superfood, 'broccoleaf' is full of antioxidants, minerals, phytonutrients and vitamins A and K. It's also higher in calcium than both kale and the broccoli florets themselves.

We hope you're seeing why we love our greens so much and swear by them!

Greens can help protect your body from illness and feed your brain. They also help to keep your skin clear, your hair shiny, your muscles lean and your digestion healthy. Essentially, they are one of the easiest ways to keep you feeling at the top of your game! Ultimately, no matter what fad diet or piece of misinformation comes your way, never give up on greens.

EAT SEASONALLY

The flavour goes up ... the nutrition goes up ... yet the price comes down: win!

There are many benefits to eating foods based on the seasons. Yes, we are blessed to live in a country where so much is available all the time, so of course you should make the most of that, but you should also try to make the most of nature. Incorporate, where you can, foods that are in season into your diet. Here's why:

✳ TASTE

It's pretty hard to argue against a juicy mango in summer that's so ripe you can smell it, compared to a mango in winter that's technically a mango but seems to lack the smell, taste and bursting flavour of its seasonal cousin.

✳ NUTRIENTS

Foods that are technically out of season have probably been stored for months (or sometimes even years!), or transported across the globe, so it's not surprising that some nutrients are lost during prolonged storage and transportation.

✳ PRICE

When produce is in season there tends to be a lot of it around, so the price comes down. Stock up!

SUMMER

Apricots * Asian greens * Bananas * Beans * Berries—
blueberries, raspberries, strawberries * Beetroot * Capsicum
(pepper) * Cauliflower * Celery * Cherries * Cucumber
Eggplant (aubergine) * Grapes * Leeks * Lettuce * Mangoes
Melons—watermelon, honeydew, rockmelon (cantaloupe)
Mushrooms * Nectarines * Peaches * Plums * Pumpkin
Silverbeet (Swiss chard) * Tomatoes

AUTUMN

Apples * Asian greens * Asparagus * Bananas * Beans
Beetroot * Berries—blueberries, raspberries, strawberries
Broccoli * Broccolini * Cabbage * Cauliflower * Cucumber
Eggplant (aubergine) * Figs * Globe artichoke * Grapes
Kale * Kiwifruit * Lemons * Lettuce * Mushrooms * Pears
Persimmons * Potatoes * Pumpkin * Quinces * Sweet corn
Tomatoes * Zucchini (courgette)

WINTER

Apples * Bananas * Broccoli * Brussels sprouts * Cauliflower
Grapefruit * Kiwifruit * Lemons * Mandarins * Mushrooms
Oranges (Navel) * Pears * Potatoes * Silverbeet (Swiss chard)

SPRING

Apples * Asparagus * Bananas * Broccoli * Brussels sprouts
Cauliflower * Celery * Fennel * Grapefruit * Leeks * Lemons
Lettuce * Mandarins * Mangoes * Mushrooms * Nectarines
Oranges (Navel) * Peas * Plums * Potatoes * Radishes
Rhubarb * Spinach * Tomatoes

SWAPS AND DROPS

If you've made our Super Green Smoothies before, or cooked up our nourishing, lean recipes from *The Good Life*, you'll know that we're pretty big on our 'healthy swaps and drops'. What does that mean? It means that in our world, biscuits (cookies), cakes and brownies can actually be healthy. Yep, we're serious! You just need to know what substitutions to make.

Throughout this recipe book you'll find that many 'regular' ingredients have been swapped for low-kilojoule (-calorie), low-carb, gluten-free, dairy-free, natural or more nutrient-dense alternatives. By doing this, we're able to enjoy the foods we love, while still getting maximum health benefits.

When using substitutes, quantities and cooking methods will sometimes need to be altered in order to create the desired taste or consistency. For example, stevia is much sweeter than sugar and therefore you won't need as much. Coconut flour absorbs water at a much higher rate than wheat flour, so you'll need to add more liquid. The recipes in this book have already accounted for these adjustments but if you're making swaps on your own, make sure you keep this in mind.

Swaps can add nutritional value to your meal, without compromising on taste.

* BUTTER

Swap with coconut oil, organic butter or avocado. Organic butter, made from the milk of cows that are not given synthetic growth or breeding hormones, is as nutrient dense as regular butter, while coconut oil is great for energy and can help to burn fat. With a very similar texture to butter, avocado is another great substitute to have on toast.

* COW'S MILK

Swap with almond milk, soy milk, coconut milk, rice milk. Cow's milk contains lactose, which doesn't always agree with everyone's digestive system. Try using one of the alternatives instead for a lower kilojoule (calorie), lactose-free, vegan option.

* LOW-FAT YOGHURT

Swap with natural yoghurt, Greek-style yoghurt or coconut yoghurt. Often low-fat or no-fat dairy products are full of added sugar to make up for the lost flavour. Natural and Greek-style yoghurt are great alternatives because they're high in protein and calcium but low in sugar. Coconut yoghurt is another nutritious option if you're trying to avoid lactose. Plus it tastes amazing!

* MILK CHOCOLATE

Swap with dark chocolate with more than 80 per cent cocoa. While milk chocolate now and then isn't terrible for you, dark chocolate is a much healthier choice. You're getting that satisfying sweet hit without needing to eat much of it. The reason for this is that dark chocolate is made with more cocoa, which contains high levels of antioxidants.

* SOFT DRINKS

Swap with kombucha, fruit-infused water or coconut water. We all know that soft drinks are no match for water but sometimes water can get a bit dull. Try a ginger and lemon kombucha if you like ginger ale, or infuse your water with berries, sliced lemons, limes or oranges, or even cucumber and basil instead.

* SUGAR

Swap with stevia, agave syrup, monk fruit sweetener, rice malt syrup or xylitol. The problem with sugar is that it has a high glycaemic index (GI), meaning it provides you with a short-lived energy surge that later results in a major crash. It is also high in kilojoules (calories), which can lead to weight gain. Try one of our suggested alternatives instead.

* TABLE SALT

Swap with sea salt, pink Himalayan salt or herbs and spices. Table salt is typically more heavily processed than sea salt and pink Himalayan salt. Herbs and spices are another great way to add flavour without increasing sodium.

* VEGETABLE OIL

Swap with coconut oil, almond oil, macadamia oil, olive oil and avocado oil. Common vegetable oils often contain omega-6 polyunsaturated fatty acids, which can be harmful to your body when consumed in excess. Not only are these oil swaps safe for your health, they're actually good for you!

* WHEAT FLOUR

Swap wheat flour with coconut flour, buckwheat flour, chickpea flour (besan) or almond meal. Flour is used in many different recipes, but ordinary white flour doesn't have much nutritional value. Try substituting one of these more nutritious options to supercharge your cakes and slices!

* WHEAT PASTA OR NOODLES

Swap with buckwheat noodles or spiralised zucchini noodles. Regular pasta contains gluten and is high in carbohydrates. While these things are fine in moderation, a bowl of pasta can often give you way more carbs than you need. Try buckwheat noodles for a gluten-free alternative or zucchini noodles for a low-carb, low-kilojoule (calorie) option.

* WHITE BREAD

Swap with dark rye bread, sourdough bread, broccoli bread or sprouted grain bread. Much like white flour and pasta, white bread isn't very nutrient dense. It can also contain hidden sugars that aren't great for your teeth (or your waistline)! The alternatives will help you get the most out of your sandwiches.

DETOX TIPS

We know how it feels when you let your healthy habits slip. Sometimes you can start the year by treating your body like a temple. Then come mid-year you've got the pizza man on speed dial and a gym membership going down the drain. We've all been there!

The truth is, detoxing shouldn't be done as a one-off process. It's something you should be generally conscious of so you can try to keep your body clean all year round! We don't mean you need to eliminate treats from your diet altogether. You can still have a glass of wine at the end of a long week or celebrate with food and friends. To us, detoxing is all about taking steps every day to keep your system clean, so that you can afford to treat yourself.

Here we've put together a list of detox tips that we like to follow, and that can help you get your insides squeaky clean again (OK, maybe not 'squeaky clean' but you get the drift). Working these into your daily routine will help to reset your system and get your health back on track. With luck, you'll feel more energised and less bloated, and your hair, skin and nails will begin to glow.

Trust us, it's so worth it! ♥

#1 START THE DAY RIGHT

We've said it once and we'll say it again, breakfast is SO important. Having a well-balanced breakfast provides you with long-lasting energy, keeps you from snacking too much and can even improve your mood. For a big hit of goodness—we're talking vitamins and nutrients for increased energy and improved digestion—try drinking one of the super green smoothies from this book as your breakfast. That huge hit of vitamins, minerals and antioxidants will have you feeling amazing all day.

#2 DRINK UP

It's common knowledge that we need to drink plenty of water. Ultimately, it's the number one way to help detox your body. Not only that, but it will help to reduce fatigue, flush out toxins, boost your immune system, cure headaches, improve your complexion and even promote weight loss. For a lot of people, getting through eight glasses in a day can seem like a battle, but it's worth the effort! We recommend infusing your water with fruit, such as blueberries or strawberries, and mint. If it tastes good, you'll end up drinking more without even noticing it.

You can also add a teaspoon of our SWIISH DELIISH Super Green Superfood Powder to your water. This powder contains more than 40 ingredients designed to give you vitamins and nutrients, a huge boost of energy and a way to cleanse your system. Plus it tastes fresh, tangy and very more-ish.

Aim to drink at least 2–2.5 litres of water a day to really flush out your body so that all your organs can function at their peak again.

#3 DO SOME SHOTS

Nope, not that kind of shot. We're talking about a detox shot! Try mixing ¼ teaspoon of lemon juice, ⅛ teaspoon of cayenne pepper, 1 teaspoon of organic apple cider vinegar and 60 ml (2 fl oz/ ¼ cup) of water. Then drink up! Apple cider vinegar will work to improve digestion, lower cholesterol levels and reduce bloating. Lemon juice will help cleanse your system and give you a vitamin C hit, while cayenne pepper can increase blood circulation and fire up your metabolism.

#4 GET MOVING

Exercising for just 30 minutes a day can help to detoxify your body, improve your mood, raise your self-confidence and even help you breathe better. It doesn't necessarily have to be an intense, heart-beating-out-of-your-chest kind of workout. It can be as simple as a power walk, a yoga class or a short weight-training session: as long as you get your heart rate up you're doing something good.

#5 MAKE IT SPICY

On top of loading up on fresh veggies and fruit, we also suggest adding herbs and spices to your food. Why? Well firstly, too much salt in your diet can lead to high blood pressure and water retention (that is, bloating). Try switching your usual salt sprinkle for herbs and spices instead to help amp up flavour levels, because this also gives you health benefits at the same time. We like to add turmeric, garlic, ginger, cayenne pepper or cinnamon.

#6 SWEAT SESSIONS

One of the easiest ways to get rid of toxins is to sweat them out. One way we like to do this is by taking an infrared sauna. Infrared saunas are special saunas that use infrared lighting to penetrate deep into the tissue. This allows the temperature of your body to rise slowly, which makes you sweat and consequently remove the build-up of unwanted toxins in your pores.

LOVE YOUR GUTS

You may not realise it, but the state of your digestive system can have a huge impact on your overall health. In fact, 90 per cent of serotonin (also known as the happy hormone) is produced in the digestive tract.

Not only does keeping your digestive system in a good state make you feel good, but it also has a whole heap of health benefits that affect every inch of your body.

Having a healthy gut can help to boost energy levels, improve memory, reduce inflammation and give you an overall sense of wellbeing. Unfortunately, a bad diet, stress and an imbalance of bacteria in the gut can lead to a digestive disaster. We're talking abdominal pain, bloating after meals, flatulence, headaches, fatigue, joint pain, moodiness and overall immune system weakness. Ah, no thanks!

We've listed a few of our top tips to help get your gut flora back to where it should be. These are the 'healthy gut rules' that you'll find can easily be applied when whipping up the recipes in this book.

* CUT THE JUNK

By this, we mean cut out as many non-nutritious foods as you can. We're not saying don't ever have a glass of wine or a slice of pizza, but cut out as much as possible of alcohol, processed foods, 'bad' fats and anything you may have an intolerance to, such as gluten or dairy. We know how hard this is, but if you want to improve your digestive health, cutting down on unnecessary foods is the first step you need to nail. These substances can irritate the gut and cause it to become inflamed, which leads to a whole lot of health problems down the track. Stick to clean eating with the recipes in this book, and you will kickstart lots of healthy habits that will make this step to gut health a whole lot easier.

* KEEP IT WHOLE

We've said it before and we'll say it again, you can't go wrong with eating whole, unprocessed foods. Eating this way is one of the major keys to good health! Your gut will love you for it. The types of foods that will help to improve your gut health are those that contain substances such as omega-3 fatty acids, amino acids such as L-glutamine, anti-oxidants and zinc. Some examples of good foods to choose include almonds, oats, garlic, asparagus, turmeric, bananas, endive and mushrooms.

* FERMENTED AND CULTURED FOODS

On top of wholefoods, eating or drinking fermented and cultured products is one of the best ways to improve digestive health. These includes things such as sauerkraut, kombucha, kimchi and kefir. These sorts of foods are filled with probiotics, which promote the growth of bacteria in the gut. They help to clean out your system in order to make you feel lighter, leaner and cleaner. Add these foods to your diet and you can say goodbye to bloating and hello to a flat, healthy, comfortable tummy. HOORAY!

* SUPER SUPPLEMENT

Sometimes, you might not have time to hunt down sauerkraut for your salad. Other times, wholefoods aren't on hand and you end up resorting to less gut-friendly fast-food options. Hey, you're only human! Or maybe you just want to amp things up a notch and make sure you're getting the biggest shot of good health that you can. This was one of the main things we had in mind when we designed our SWIISH DELIISH Super Green Superfood Powder, which you'll find in our SWIISH online store (shop. swiish.com). With a delicious blend of 40 ingredients, including those all-important green veggies, probiotics and superfoods, this powder is designed to keep your gut in good shape even on the days you slip up. It may also help to boost your energy levels and detoxify your system. It's been a total game-changer for us, and for so many others!

* DRINK UP

Drinking enough water is crucial if you want to maintain good gut health. This is because water helps to break down food so that your body can absorb the nutrients easily. Water also cleanses your digestive system, which allows it to function at its best.

* MAKE SURE YOU MOVE

Exercising for at least 30 minutes each day will help to keep your digestive system running smoothly. This will strengthen the muscles in your abdomen and allow your intestines to contract properly, which can help to move food through your system. Along with yoga, it can also help to reduce stress.

* DE-STRESS

Believe it or not, the number one reason that things go wrong with your gut is stress. When you get stressed out, this causes your nervous system to go into 'fight or flight' mode. This is unfortunately very bad for your digestive system, as it causes the blood to flow away from your gut and into the bigger muscle groups (the ones needed to run away from danger). Working yoga or meditation into your weekly routine can help to reduce stress and ultimately improve your digestive health.

Believe it or not, the number one reason that things go wrong with your gut is stress.

TURMERIC AND GINGER BREW

DF // GF // NF // SF // V // VG // P // 79 KJ/19 CAL PER SERVE // SERVES 1

1 teaspoon grated fresh ginger
1 teaspoon dried turmeric
    (grated fresh turmeric root is
    also fine)
juice of ½ a medium lemon
250 ml (9 fl oz/1 cup) of hot
    (boiled) water
½ teaspoon stevia (or more
    to taste)

Combine all the ingredients in a mug, stirring
well. Add more stevia (or rice malt syrup or honey)
if desired.

NOTE

* To ensure the maximum absorption of the nutrients
  from the turmeric, make sure the water isn't boiling
  when you make the brew.

This is one of our favourite immunity-boosting drinks. It's very warm and soothing, particularly if you're feeling run-down.

FREQUENTLY ASKED QUESTIONS

Q: I am trying to lose weight. What approach would you recommend I take, in order to shed a few kilos?

A: **Losing weight is a common goal for many people.** The first thing we would recommend is to always consult a doctor before starting any type of weight-loss regimen. Throughout this recipe book we include the kilojoule (calorie) count for all our meals. Since you are looking to lose weight, we recommend choosing a few meals that will add up to 6275 kilojoules (1500 calories) a day, before shifting to a 5000-kilojoule (1195-calorie) meal plan when you feel ready. It's also important to get in around half an hour of movement every day. Try going for a long walk, taking a bike ride or swimming laps.

Q: Why do you have smoothies?

A: **Well, having a smoothie a day is one of the easiest, simplest changes** we made to our diet, and what we gained in return was weight loss, more energy, clearer skin, shinier hair, better sleep, improved digestion and immunity, and a whole lot of nutrients. We also found it removed our cravings for sugar and processed foods. There is no way we could sit down and eat this many greens in one go, so blending them is the perfect solution.

Q: What is the difference between juice and a smoothie?

A: **Both juices and smoothies are great for your health.** A juice contains only the liquid extracted from a fruit or vegetable, and although it contains very little dietary fibre it still contains vitamins and nutrients. A smoothie, on the other hand, has the lot: fibre, vitamins and nutrients.

Q: Can I replace a meal with a smoothie?

A: **Yes, you definitely can.** We would suggest you replace a meal where you tend to make poor choices or struggle to eat well. For us, during the week that meal is breakfast, simply because we're trying to get dressed, ready and out the door. It's different for everyone. We have a friend who used to struggle to eat well at dinner. She confessed to wandering back and forth between the fridge and the pantry, aimlessly eating whatever she could get her hands on. For her, having a smoothie for dinner has been a game-changer. She's lost 8 kilograms (17½ lb), she's sleeping better and she's feeling the best she's felt in a long time.

This is such a great question which we are often asked.

Q: What time of day is best to have a smoothie?

A: **Whatever time you want.** There is no 'best' time: you can have one for breakfast, lunch, dinner or as a snack during the day.

Q: Why are greens so important?

A: **Green vegetables are high in vitamins and minerals, fibre, proteins, antioxidants**, fat-burning compounds and healthy bacteria. They are also low in kilojoules (calories). The nutrients from green leafy vegetables can help protect your body from illness, cleanse your kidneys and feed your brain. They help your body maintain good health, clearer skin and shinier hair, build leaner muscles and ensure healthy digestion.

Q: Are the recipes in this book paleo-friendly?

A: **Many recipes in this book are paleo-friendly.** A paleo diet is full of fresh, unprocessed foods but avoids dairy, legumes, grains, processed foods and refined sugar, all of which is very much in line with our food philosophy. While we enjoy legumes and grains, if you're following a strict paleo regimen, look for recipes marked paleo at the top of the page.

Q: Can I use frozen ingredients in my smoothies?

A: **Yes! Most of your ingredients can be frozen.** In particular, baby spinach, kale, broccoli, bananas, pineapple, mango and berries. It's nice to have at least one frozen ingredient in your smoothie because cold ingredients make your smoothie taste better.

Q: I don't have time to make a smoothie every day. Can I make a bigger batch and refrigerate or freeze it?

A: **Yes. Smoothies only last in the fridge for about 24 hours.** After that, they lose some nutrients and won't taste as fresh; however, you can freeze smoothies. We suggest that if you want to do this, freeze them in daily portions in some airtight containers or jars (just be careful to leave some space at the top of the jar as the smoothie will expand in the freezer). Defrost your smoothie in the fridge the night before you want to drink it, and it'll be thawed and ready to go by morning. You'll find it needs a little chlorophyll, lemon, lime or herbs to give it a fresh shot of zing and an added flavour boost.

Q: What type of blender should I buy to make my smoothies?

A: **A blender is a great kitchen essential that can be used for many different purposes**—soups, dips and, of course, smoothies—so it is a good investment; however, you don't need to spend a heap of money to make great smoothies. If you already have a blender, try it out and see how you go using it to make smoothies. You might need to adjust your ingredients slightly to get the right consistency. We suggest using a little more liquid and blending your greens and liquid first before adding the remaining ingredients. You may also need to add ingredients gradually so that you don't overpower the motor of the blender, or add a little more liquid to achieve the right consistency, which may be necessary no what matter what type of blender you own. The most important thing to do is just start. After all, you can always upgrade later.

Q: My green smoothie turned brown. Is this normal?

A: **Sometimes mixing fruits like straw-berries or watermelon with green leafy vegetables will turn your smoothie brown.** Don't worry—it will still taste good. But if you really don't like the colour, try adding dark berries to make it purple.

Q: Can green smoothies help with weight loss?

A: **Absolutely! If you want to lose weight, green smoothies are such a good way to go.** They can kickstart your digestion, reduce bad cholesterol, increase your energy, regulate and improve bowel movements, help you burn excess fat and decrease cravings for processed, sugary foods. Smoothies are packed with nutrients, vitamins and fibre. They're filling and they taste great, making it an easy lifestyle change to make.

You're not eating processed 'diet' food. Rather, you're consuming real food. Living food. Good food. Food that nourishes. Most of us have started a diet on Monday only to find ourselves binge-eating wildly like a half-starved animal by Wednesday. Because smoothies taste great and are easy to make, they offer a sustainable weight-loss method when combined with a balanced, nutritious diet and exercise.

Q: I'm worried my smoothie will taste bitter from all the spinach and kale but I'd prefer not to add any sugars. How can I fix this?

A: **The easiest way to reduce the bitterness is to add lemon or lime.** A small squeeze should do the trick, but add more if it's needed.

Q: I'm really busy and often don't have a lot of time to prepare meals. Are your recipes quick and easy to follow?

A: **Almost all the recipes are easy and simple to prepare so you won't need to be in the kitchen for hours on end.** Of all the recipes, smoothies will be the quickest to prepare, so these are a great option if you're rushed in the morning. While some of the salads and bowls require you to cook a couple of things, we try to keep it as simple as possible. That's what the book is all about! We also like to use microwave rice and quinoa to speed things up. Check our Super + Simple Tips (see page 10) for more.

Q: I've heard a lot about the dangers of too much sugar in the diet. Are your recipes free of refined sugar?

A: **Almost all the recipes in this book contain no refined sugar** (such as refined white sugar). For the most part, we have used natural sweeteners or sugar substitutes in recipes where a little sweetening is required.

Q: Can you suggest any low-sugar fruit options to replace banana?

A: **We use bananas in our smoothies because they provide the perfect dense, creamy base**; however, if you don't like bananas or prefer a low-sugar substitute, you can try using berries, pear, apple, peach, melons such as rockmelon (cantaloupe), honeydew or watermelon, nectarines, puréed pumpkin, frozen peas or avocado instead. These will keep your smoothie tasty without the sugar spike.

Q: I'm trying to avoid gluten. Can this recipe book accommodate that?

A: **There are lots of gluten-free recipes in this book.** To make things easier for readers, there are labels at the top of each recipe to indicate whether it is paleo-friendly, gluten-free, dairy-free, sugar-free, nut-free, vegan, vegetarian or all of the above.

Q: There are some ingredients listed in your recipes that I've never bought before. Where is the best place to look?

A: **We use a lot of superfoods.** Some of them you may have heard of and some of them are fresh on the health-food scene. The good news is that most, if not all, are available from supermarkets or health-food stores. They might cost a little bit more but we believe that it's better to invest in good health now, and live the best life you can.

Q: If I have an allergy or intolerance to something, am I able to swap that ingredient out?

A: **Of course! Typical allergies include things like nuts and seafood, while intolerances often include things like gluten, dairy and soy.** If nuts are an issue for you, simply omit them from the recipe. You may like to try substitutes such as pumpkin seeds (pepitas), sesame seeds or even chia seeds. If a recipe calls for nut butter, try using tahini instead. If a recipe contains gluten, you can always swap for gluten-free substitutes such as buckwheat pasta, brown rice and gluten-free bread or flour.

Q: I keep hearing that being 'alkaline' is good for your health. What does this mean and how can I become alkaline?

A: **Basically, alkaline is the internal state in which your immune system, your cells and all the chemical reactions inside them are working with maximum efficiency.** Your body is said to be at its healthiest when your insides are working in an alkaline environment, as opposed to an acidic one. The fastest way to get alkaline is to up your daily veggie intake as much as you can. Dietitians recommend you eat about 5–7 servings of vegetables daily. Enjoy a smoothie plus one of our super-food salads or smoothie brekkie bowls each day and your body will quickly become more alkaline.

Q: I'm a vegetarian. Are there options in this recipe book for me?

A: **Of course! There are lots of vegetarian recipes to choose from in this book.** If a recipe that you like calls for meat, you also have the option to swap this for a vegetarian alternative such as eggs, tofu, lentils, chickpeas, tempeh or cooked beans. Keep in mind that cooking times will vary for these ingredients.

Q: Doesn't it take a long time to make a smoothie?

A: **Making a smoothie only takes a few minutes; preparation is the key.** If you're always on the go, wash, chop and freeze your ingredients in advance. We keep fruit and vegetable ingredients in resealable bags in the freezer, so that we can use them at any time.

Q: Can I make green smoothies for my kids?

A: **Yes. We often try to sneak greens into our kids' meals and this is a great way for the little ones to get lots of tasty goodness in a glass.** The only exception is if a smoothie calls for matcha powder, green tea or coffee (as these contain caffeine), or protein powder, neither of which is designed to be consumed by children. Simply omit these ingredients if they are in the recipe.

Q: Why do you use almond milk in your smoothies?

A: **Almond milk is a great source of protein; it's low in kilojoules (calories) and ticks the box for those who want to eat dairy-free.** You can also use rice, oat or quinoa milk if you like. If you prefer to go for cow's milk, you can use full fat or skim. If you like soy, that's OK too. It's totally up to you and your taste buds. Sometimes, if we want to keep it to just the fruit, veggies and superfoods, we use water in the recipes instead.

Check out this amazing layered smoothie on page 70.

– CHAPTER ONE –

smoothies

GIMME A LITTLE ZING BOWL

GF // NF // VG // 1644 KJ/393 CAL PER SERVE // SERVES 1
820 KJ/196 CAL PER SERVE // SERVES 2

250 ml (9 fl oz/1 cup)
    unsweetened coconut milk
    (carton variety)
70 g (2½ oz/¼ cup) Greek-
    style yoghurt
90 g (3¼ oz/2 cups) baby
    spinach leaves
10 g (⅓ oz/¼ cup) rocket
    (aragula) leaves
15 g (½ oz/¼ cup) broccoli
    florets
¼ medium avocado
190 g (6½ oz/1 cup) chopped
    pineapple
1 large kiwifruit, skin removed
1 teaspoon honey (more to
    taste)

Put all the ingredients into a blender and process until smooth. Once blended, pour into a bowl and top with your desired toppings.

We've used:

* frozen raspberries
* kiwi fruit
* dragonfruit
* star fruit
* desiccated (shredded) coconut

RESTORE SMOOTHIE

NF // SF // VG // 998 KJ/238 CAL PER SERVE // SERVES 2

250 ml (9 fl oz/1 cup)
   unsweetened almond milk
130 g (4½ oz/½ cup) vanilla-
   flavoured yoghurt
155 g (5½ oz/1 cup) frozen
   blueberries
1 teaspoon chia seeds
2 teaspoons rice malt syrup
½ teaspoon vanilla extract
   or ¼ teaspoon vanilla
   bean paste
50 g (1¾ oz/½ cup) rolled
   (porridge) oats
½ banana, sliced, to serve
   (optional)
honey to serve (optional)

Put all the ingredients except the oats into a blender and process until smooth.

Add the oats and blend lightly to retain the thickness.

Pour into a jar or glass and, if topping the smoothie with sliced banana, first leave it to thicken for about 20–30 minutes. Drizzle with honey if desired.

TIP

✳ You can make the smoothie the night before and then top with the banana slices immediately before serving.

THE ALL-VEGGIE ALL-ROUNDER

DF // GF // NF // SF // V // VG // P // 644 KJ/154 CAL PER SERVE // SERVES 1

375 ml (13 fl oz/1½ cups)
    coconut water
15 g (½ oz/½ cup) kale ribbons
    (stalks removed, leaves
    sliced)
25 g (¾ oz/½ cup) chopped
    cos (romaine) lettuce
½ small zucchini (courgette),
    skin on
1 teaspoon coconut oil

Put all the ingredients into a blender and process
until smooth.

We couldn't pack any more
into this smoothie bowl if we tried!

BERRY DELICIOUS BOWL

GF // SF // VG // 1006 KJ/240 CAL PER SERVE // SERVES 2

45 g (1½ oz/1 cup) baby
    spinach leaves
25 g (1 oz/1 cup) kale ribbons
    (stalks removed, leaves
    sliced)
30 g (1 oz/¼ cup) cauliflower
    florets
15 g (½ oz/¼ cup) broccoli
    florets
½ frozen banana
220 g (8 oz/1 cup) frozen
    mixed berries
3 medjool dates, pitted
70 g (2½ oz/¼ cup) Greek-
    style yoghurt
250 ml (9 fl oz/1 cup)
    unsweetened almond milk

Put all the ingredients into a blender and process until smooth.

Pour into a bowl and add the toppings of your choice.

We've used:

* millet puffs
* chia seeds
* toasted coconut flakes or desiccated (shredded) coconut
* fresh berries
* banana slices
* dragonfruit
* edible flowers (dianthus)

IT TAKES TWO TO MANGO WHIPPED SMOOTHIE

DF // GF // NF // SF // V // VG // P // 1284 KJ/307 CAL PER SERVE // SERVES 2

1 frozen banana
315 g (11¼ oz/1 cup) frozen
  mango pieces
120 g (4¼ oz/1 cup) frozen
  cauliflower florets

Put all the ingredients into a food processor and blend.

You will see that the ingredients start out a bit crumbly; just keep blending until it comes together into a whip.

Add the toppings of your choice.

We've used:
* pomegranate seeds
* desiccated (shredded) coconut
* mango cheek, peeled and sliced

chia squad

hot chocolate

CHIA SQUAD

DF // GF // SF // V // VG // P // 1163 KJ/278 CAL PER SERVE // SERVES 1

45 g (1½ oz/1 cup) baby
    spinach leaves
15 g (½ oz/½ cup) kale ribbons
    (stalks removed, leaves
    sliced)
185 g (6½ oz/1 cup) chopped
    mango
375 ml (13 fl oz/1½ cups)
    unsweetened vanilla
    almond milk
1½ tablespoons chia seeds
stevia, to taste

Put all the ingredients into a blender. Blend to the desired consistency.

HOT CHOCOLATE

GF // NF // SF // V // VG // P // 1201 KJ/287 CAL PER SERVE // SERVES 1

250 ml (9 fl oz/1 cup) skim milk
90 g (3¼ oz/2 cups) baby
    spinach leaves
1 frozen banana
125 g (4½ oz/1 cup) raspberries
1 tablespoon cacao powder
¼ teaspoon chilli powder

Put all the ingredients into a blender and process until smooth.

NEAPOLITAN LAYERED SMOOTHIE

DF // GF // SF // V // VG // P // 1410 KJ/337 CAL PER SERVE // SERVES 4

190 g (6¾ oz/1 cup)
  buckwheat, soaked in water
  for 2 hours

BASE LAYER
125 ml (4 fl oz/½ cup)
  unsweetened almond milk
1 frozen banana
235 g (8½ oz/1½ cups) frozen
  blueberries

MIDDLE LAYER
125 ml (4 fl oz/½ cup)
  unsweetened almond milk
2 frozen bananas

TOP LAYER
125 ml (4 fl oz/½ cup)
  unsweetened almond milk
1 frozen banana
190 g (6½ oz/1½ cups) frozen
  raspberries

Blend all the ingredients for the base layer in a food processor or blender. Drain the buckwheat and add half, stirring well. This will allow the smoothie to thicken.

Pour the base layer into 4 jars or cups and place in the freezer for 10 minutes to set.

Blend all the ingredients for the middle layer. Add half the remaining buckwheat and stir well. Pour over the base layer and return to the freezer for 10 minutes to set.

Blend all the ingredients for the top layer. Add the remaining buckwheat and stir well. Pour over the white layer.

Add your desired toppings. We've used raspberries, millet puffs and desiccated (shredded) coconut.

NOTE
* We add buckwheat for two reasons: one is that it allows the smoothie to thicken, making it easier to create layers. The second is that buckwheat is amazing for you (see page 32).

Buckwheat is perfect for creating layers as it thickens beautifully.

SKINNY PASSION POWER SMOOTHIE

DF // GF // NF // SF // V // VG // P // 912 KJ/218 CAL PER SERVE // SERVES 1

250 ml (9 fl oz/1 cup) water
15 g (½ oz/½ cup) kale ribbons
    (stalks removed, leaves
    sliced)
45 g (1½ oz/1 cup) baby
    spinach leaves
1 small Lebanese (short)
    cucumber
1 orange, peeled and seeded
1 frozen banana
2 passionfruit, plus extra to
    serve (optional)

Put all the ingredients except for the passionfruit into a blender. Process until smooth.

Stir in the passionfruit pulp and seeds at the end.

Top with additional passionfruit if desired.

SWEET DREAMS SMOOTHIE

DF // SF // V // VG // P // 1121 KJ/268 CAL PER SERVE // SERVES 1–2

250 ml (9 fl oz/1 cup) brewed chamomile tea

7 g (¼ oz/¼ cup) kale ribbons (stalks removed, leaves sliced)

25 g (1 oz/¼ cup) rolled (porridge) oats

150 g (5½ oz/1 cup) frozen pitted cherries

1 teaspoon almond butter

Put all the ingredients into a blender and process for 2 minutes or until smooth.

WHY THIS SMOOTHIE WORKS ...

* *Chamomile* is a mild sedative.

* *Kale* is loaded with calcium, which helps the brain use tryptophan to manufacture melatonin. Melatonin is a natural hormone produced by the pineal gland in the brain. It helps to induce and regulate sleep.

* *Cherries* are rich in melatonin, which fuels the body for rest.

* *Almonds* contain tryptophan and magnesium, which help to relax muscles.

Definitely Instagram worthy!

GREEN SUPREME LAYERED SMOOTHIE

DF // GF // V // VG // P // 1526 KJ/364 CAL PER SERVE // SERVES 3

270 g (9 oz/6 cups) frozen
   baby spinach leaves
3 frozen bananas
945 g (2 lb/3 cups) frozen
   mango pieces
750 ml (27 fl oz/3 cups)
   unsweetened vanilla
   almond milk, plus 250 ml
   (9 fl oz/1 cup) unsweetened
   vanilla almond milk extra

Place the spinach, banana, mango and 3 cups of almond milk in a blender and blend until smooth. Divide the mixture into three portions.

Divide portion 1 across three jars and freeze for 2 hours.

While portion 1 freezes, take portion 2 and add ¼ cup vanilla almond milk. Pour portion 2 on top of portion 1 in each jar and return it to the freezer.

Take portion 3 and add the remaining ¾ cup of vanilla almond milk. Pour portion 3 on top of portion 2 in each jar and freeze until firm.

Top as desired.

We've used:
* paleo granola
* blackberries
* pumpkin seeds (pepitas)
* star fruit
* honey
* goji berries

CHOC FULL OF VEGGIES WHIPPED BOWL

DF // GF // NF // SF // V // VG // P // 1084 KJ/259 CAL PER SERVE // SERVES 2

¼ avocado
60 g (2 oz/1 cup) frozen broccoli
45 g (1½ oz/1 cup) frozen baby spinach leaves
1 frozen banana
4 medjool dates
2 tablespoons unsweetened cocoa powder

Put all the ingredients into a food processor and blend.

You will see that the ingredients start out a bit crumbly; just keep blending until it comes together into a whip.

Add the toppings of your choice.

We've used:
* cacao nibs
* fresh raspberries
* fresh fig slices
* dusting of cacao powder
* edible flowers (such as dianthus)

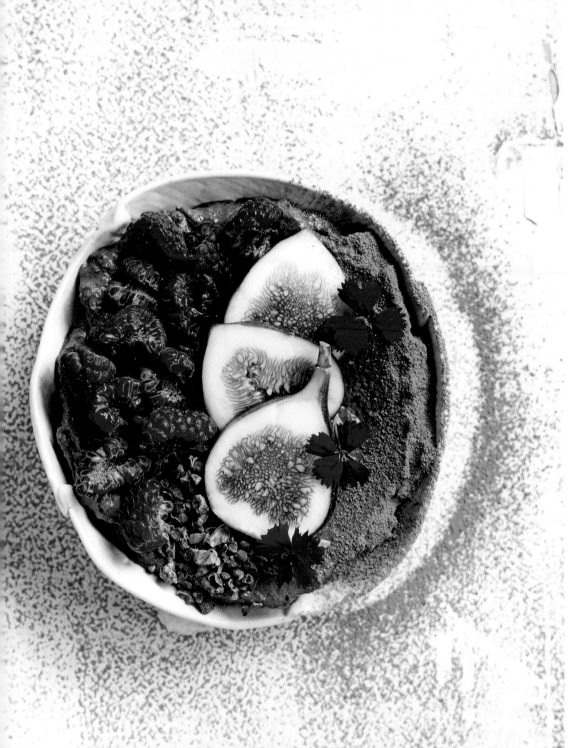

FUEL UP YOUR SMOOTHIE FOR A WORKOUT

✳ ACAI BERRY

The acai berry is an energy-boosting fruit so it's perfect for a pre-workout boost.

✳ OATS

Slow-releasing rolled (porridge) oats top our pre-workout smoothie list because they'll give you long-lasting energy. Soak them if you have time, but we usually just add them dry.

✳ BANANA

Loaded with potassium and antioxidants, banana packs one of the greatest nutrient punches, providing a solid pre-workout boost.

✳ COCONUT OIL

Another great choice pre-workout—it's easily absorbed by the body and quickly converted into energy.

you've got kale

the pure cure

THE PURE CURE

GF // VG // 1418 KJ/339 CAL PER SERVE // SERVES 1

375 ml (13 fl oz/1½ cups)
  unsweetened vanilla
  almond milk
125 g (4½ oz/1 cup) cauliflower
  florets
2 carrots
8 almonds
¼ teaspoon ground cinnamon
¼ teaspoon ground nutmeg
70 g (2½ oz/¼ cup) Greek-
  style yoghurt
1 teaspoon agave syrup (or
  more, to taste)
1 vanilla bean, seeds scraped

Put all the ingredients into a blender and pulse until blended to desired consistency. Before serving, we garnished ours by dipping the rim of the glass in some honey, then in some black chia seeds.

NOTES

❋ *Carrots are full of health benefits* from vitamins, fibre and antioxidants. Cauliflower is anti-inflammatory, antioxidant-rich and assists in detoxing. This smoothie is a double hit of the good stuff, mixed in with cinnamon, which is known to lower blood-sugar levels and help reduce the risk of heart disease, and nutmeg, which increases immunity, boosts skin health, relieves pain and detoxes the body. Doesn't get much better than that!

YOU'VE GOT KALE

DF // GF // NF // VG // P // 816 KJ/195 CAL PER SERVE // SERVES 1

250 ml (9 fl oz/1 cup) coconut
  water
125 ml (4 fl oz/½ cup) water
45 g (1½ oz/1 cup) baby
  spinach leaves
15 g (½ oz/½ cup) kale ribbons
  (stalks removed, leaves sliced)
½ Lebanese (short) cucumber
2 kiwifruit, peeled
1 teaspoon honey

Put all the ingredients into a blender and process until smooth. Before serving, we garnished ours by dipping the rim of the glass in some honey, then in some millet puffs.

ALL WHITE ALL RIGHT

GF // NF // SF // VG // 640 KJ/153 CAL PER SERVE // SERVES 1

125 ml (4½ oz/½ cup) skim milk
½ fresh banana
120 g (4¼ oz/1 cup) frozen
    cauliflower florets
80 g (3 oz/½ cup) frozen
    pineapple chunks

Blend all the ingredients until smooth. Pour into a bowl, then garnish with your desired toppings.

We've used:
* mango chunks
* honeydew melon
* star fruit
* quinoa puffs
* honeycomb
* shredded coconut

PRETTY IN PINK

GF // NF // SF // VG // 1619 KJ/387 CAL PER SERVE // SERVES 1

300 g (10½ oz/2 cups) frozen
    strawberries
150 g (5½ oz/1 cup) frozen
    pitted cherries
25 g (1 oz/½ cup) baby
    spinach leaves
½ frozen banana
60 ml (2 fl oz/¼ cup)
    unsweetened coconut milk
    (carton variety; you may
    need a little extra to achieve
    your desired texture for the
    bowl)
130 g (4½ oz/½ cup) yoghurt

Blend all the ingredients until smooth. Pour into a bowl, then garnish with your desired toppings.

We've used:
* watermelon
* frozen cherries
* frozen raspberries
* blueberries
* edible flowers
* granola

all white all right

pretty in pink

THE PURIST

DF // GF // NF // SF // V // VG // P // 607 KJ/145 CAL PER SERVE // SERVES 1

375 ml (13 fl oz/1½ cups) water
½ Lebanese (short) cucumber
65 g (2½ oz/1½ cups) baby
    spinach leaves
½ lime, skin on
½ small avocado, peeled and
    stone removed
7 g (¼ oz/¼ cup) mint leaves
10 g (⅓ oz/⅓ cup) basil leaves
small pinch cayenne pepper
    (optional)

Blend the water, cucumber, spinach, lime and avocado in a food processor.

Add the remaining ingredients and blend again until smooth.

'AVO GREAT DAY GREEN BOWL

DF // GF // SF // V // VG // P // 1217 KJ/291 CAL PER SERVE // SERVES 1

250 ml (9 fl oz/1 cup)
  unsweetened almond milk
90 g (3¼ oz/2 cups) baby
  spinach leaves
15 g (½ oz/½ cup) kale ribbons
  (stalks removed, leaves
  sliced)
1 large frozen banana
¼ medium avocado
1 teaspoon almond butter
stevia, to taste (optional)

Put all the ingredients into a blender and process until smooth, then top with your desired toppings.

We've used:
* avocado slices
* baby spinach leaves
* pumpkin seeds (pepitas)
* goji berries
* cacao nibs
* pistachios
* desiccated (shredded) coconut
* chia seeds
* sunflower seeds

ACAI WHAT YOU DID THERE BOWL

DF // GF // NF // SF // V // VG // P // 945 KJ/226 CAL PER SERVE // SERVES 2

BASE LAYER
220 g (8 oz/1 cup) frozen
mixed berries

CHIA PUDDING LAYER
250 ml (9 fl oz/1 cup)
unsweetened coconut milk
(carton variety)
2 tablespoons desiccated
(shredded) coconut
3 tablespoons chia seeds
2 teaspoons stevia

ACAI LAYER
100 g (3½ oz) frozen acai
berries

Put all the ingredients for the chia pudding in a mixing bowl and stir well to combine. Cover with plastic wrap and leave to set in the fridge for 3–4 hours or, better yet, overnight.

Roughly chop the mixed berries and mash with a fork. Put the berries as the base layer at the bottom of two jars (or glasses). Spoon the chia pudding over the base layer.

Blend the frozen acai berries in a food processor or blender and layer over the chia pudding.

Garnish with your desired toppings.

We've used:
* millet puffs
* desiccated (shredded) coconut
* fresh blueberries
* mint leaves

DETOX-DEBLOAT-ENERGISER

DF // GF // NF // SF // V // VG // P // 648 KJ/155 CAL PER SERVE // SERVES 1

250 ml (9 fl oz/1 cup) coconut
   water
60 ml (2 fl oz/¼ cup)
   unsweetened coconut milk
   (carton variety)
65 g (2½ oz/1½ cups) baby
   spinach leaves
½ small Lebanese (short)
   cucumber
120 g (4¼ oz/¾ cup) chopped
   pineapple
15 g (½ oz/¼ cup) coarsely
   chopped broccoli florets
¼ frozen lime, skin on
1 teaspoon SWIISH DELIISH
   Super Green Superfood
   Powder

Put all the ingredients into a blender and process
until smooth.

A spoonful of the SWIISH DELIISH Super Green Superfood Powder in this smoothie makes it the ultimate extra pick-me-up!

skinny detox

skin deep

SKINNY DETOX

DF // GF // NF // SF // V // VG // P // 920 KJ/220 CAL PER SERVE // SERVES 1

90 g (3¼ oz/2 cups) baby
    spinach leaves
30 g (1 oz/½ cup) broccoli
    florets
1 ruby red grapefruit
½ frozen banana
250 ml (9 fl oz/1 cup) coconut
    water
10 g (⅓ oz/⅓ cup) basil leaves

Put all the ingredients into a blender and process
until smooth. We garnished ours with edible flowers
(dianthus) and basil.

SKIN DEEP

DF // GF // SF // V // VG // P // 954 KJ/228 CAL PER SERVE // SERVES 1

250 ml (9 fl oz/1 cup)
    unsweetened almond milk
25 g (1 oz/1 cup) kale ribbons
    (stalks removed, leaves
    sliced)
220 g (7¾ oz/1 cup) mixed
    berries
45 g (1½ oz/¼ cup) seedless
    red grapes
12½ g (½ oz/¼ cup) chopped
    baby cos (romaine) lettuce
1 tablespoon chia seeds

Put all the ingredients into a blender and process
until smooth, then garnish with the toppings of
your choice.

We've used:
* dragonfruit
* cherries
* desiccated (shredded) coconut

LAYER CAKE SMOOTHIE

GF // SF // VG // 1242 KJ/297 CAL PER SERVE // SERVES 4

LAYER 1: PURPLE SMOOTHIE LAYER

155 g (5½ oz/1 cup) frozen
    blueberries
½ fresh banana

LAYER 2: PINK SMOOTHIE LAYER

150 g (5½ oz/1 cup) frozen
    raspberries
½ fresh banana
1 tablespoon Greek-style
    yoghurt

LAYER 3: GREEN SMOOTHIE LAYER

90 g (3¼ oz/2 cups) frozen
    baby spinach leaves
315 g (11¼ oz/1 cup) frozen
    avocado chunks
125 ml (4 fl oz/½ cup)
    unsweetened almond milk
2 medjool dates
½ teaspoon stevia

LAYER 4: YELLOW SMOOTHIE LAYER

160 g (6 oz/1 cup) frozen
    pineapple chunks
1 fresh banana

Blend all the ingredients for the base layer and pour into four jars (or glasses).

Place the jars in the freezer while you blend the next layer. Do this each time, to ensure that the smoothie stays frozen while you create the next colour.

Blend all the ingredients for the next layer, then freeze and continue this process until all the layers are done.

Top as desired. We've used pineapple wedges and frozen cherries, strawberries and blackberries.

NOTE

* *This is a thick smoothie.* We usually do this as a SERVES 4 and put them in small jars so each person gets a full colour spectrum but in a more manageable quantity.

MAKE YOUR SMOOTHIE INSTAGRAM WORTHY

For the record, our priority is that every smoothie is health, wellness, vitality and energy worthy. Still, we get it: if no one saw it on Instagram, did it even happen at all? Ha ha! Here are some tips to make your smoothies both snap ready and swoon worthy.

✳ CONSISTENCY

The edible flowers and pomegranate seeds that sit on top of the smoothie bowls don't sink because the smoothie has a thick consistency. So if you are taking a picture of a smoothie bowl, you'll want it to be a bit thicker, so don't overblend. If you have blended too much, try to salvage it by adding chia seeds: they're great for you, plus they will swell and thicken the smoothie.

✳ SYMMETRY

When you lay your garnish on top of smoothie bowls, symmetry works well. Rows of chia seeds, followed by rows of blueberries, followed by rows of kiwifruit work well. It's clean and simple and allows each row to really pop.

✳ CREATIVITY

OK, so ignore everything we said above and do the exact opposite, because that works well too! Randomness and splattering of toppings can also look great. If you opt for this method then ensure you have a mix of textures, such as flaked almonds, which are hard, and edible flowers, which are soft. You'll also want a mix of coloured toppings, and don't forget to cover only part of the bowl, so that the smoothie can still be seen.

✳ BACKGROUND

Keep the background and the base of your photo simple. A wooden board, marble plate or a linen napkin under-neath work well. Opt for a light-coloured bowl—white or pale grey or blue—as it will make the smoothie stand out.

✳ FOLLOW THE LIGHT

You need natural light. Flash is the death of a great smoothie photo. If it's night-time then our best advice is enjoy the smoothie and forget the photo.

✳ BE QUICK

Smoothies fade fast, so if you are decorating them don't faff around, do it quickly. Also, if you are getting props such as straws or napkins or spoons for your photo, have them ready beforehand so that once the smoothie is ready you can just place it and snap it. You could even do a trial shot with an empty smoothie bowl or jar to check you're happy with your prop placement (no one said it was easy!).

✳ WHICH IS MY BEST SIDE?

Always try a couple of angles: from the side, overhead, close up. It's different for every smoothie, depending on the toppings and textures and also the props and the lighting, so try a few but remember, rapid-fire photos!

✳ LAYERED SMOOTHIE TIPS AND TRICKS

DISCLAIMER: These are tricky, no question, and also time-consuming, but if neither of those things puts you off then who are we to stop you? Here are a few tips to make it a bit easier.

* Chia seeds can be used to thicken smoothies. They make things a little more solid, so they're easier to layer. Stir them in after blending the rest of the ingredients.
* Frozen fruits and vegetables blend better than fresh ones. It's best to use all frozen ingredients as it makes it easier to work with them.
* When you are starting out, begin with a two-layer smoothie. Multiple layers require quite a bit of time (and patience), so work your way up to that.

* As you do each layer, put it in the freezer to solidify, which will allow you to pour the next layer over it without the colours bleeding into each other.
* The trick to the perfect layered smoothie is to start your layers with the heaviest, densest blend at the bottom of the glass.
* Using a funnel will also allow you to pour the smoothie in slowly so that the layer underneath isn't disrupted.
* If it doesn't work, don't worry! Drink it and enjoy it and rest in the knowledge that your body and your health doesn't care if the smoothie was Instagrammed or not ... you will still reap ALL the important benefits.

SKINNY AND SWIISH WHIPPED SUPERFOOD BOWL

DF // GF // NF // SF // V // VG // P // 443 KJ/106 CAL PER SERVE // SERVES 2

2 frozen bananas
40 g (1½ oz/¼ cup) frozen
  chopped pineapple
1 teaspoon lime juice
zest of ½ lime
2 teaspoons SWIISH DELIISH
  Super Green Superfood
  Powder

Put all the ingredients into a food processor and blend. You will see that the ingredients start out a bit crumbly; just keep blending until it comes together into a whip.

TIP

* Get all your ingredients ready before you start: you'll want to ensure that everything goes into the blender frozen, as that will produce the best consistency.

NOTES

* Tinned pineapple is fine, but rinse it first.

* Our SWIISH DELIISH Super Green Superfood Powder contains more than 40 different fruits, vegetables, superfoods and probiotics. It also has a deliciously refreshing pine–lime flavour, and we've amped up this recipe with the lime juice and rind. If you already have another green superfood powder blend you can use that, but the flavour will be different. Ours is available from shop.swiish.com.

ISLAND DREAMING SMOOTHIE BOWL

DF // GF // NF // SF // V // VG // P // 1201 KJ/287 CAL PER SERVE // SERVES 1

250 ml (9 fl oz/1 cup) coconut water

90 g (3 oz/2 cups) baby spinach leaves

315 g (11¼ oz/1 cup) frozen mango pieces

¼ lime, peeled and seeds removed

7 g (¼ oz/¼ cup) mint leaves

1 teaspoon stevia, more to taste

Put all the ingredients into a blender and process until smooth, then top with your desired toppings.

We've used:

* passionfruit
* frozen mango pieces
* mint leaves
* desiccated (shredded) coconut
* lime zest
* pineapple wedges

GUILT-FREE STICKY DATE SMOOTHIE

DF // GF // SF // V // VG // P // 1477 KJ/353 CAL PER SERVE // SERVES 1

250 ml (9 fl oz/1 cup) unsweetened vanilla almond milk
90 g (3¼ oz/2 cups) baby spinach leaves
1 teaspoon almond butter
3 medjool dates, pitted
½ frozen banana
60 g (2¼ oz/½ cup) coarsely chopped cauliflower florets
pinch of ground cinnamon (optional)

Put all the ingredients into a blender and process until smooth.

NOTE

* We'd never just throw the term 'sticky date' around loosely. Trust us, we take sticky date seriously! This smoothie has the sticky date goodness you'd expect from a sticky date pudding but you won't be able to get over the fact that it's full of vegetables.

ULTIMATE FIGHTER

DF // GF // NF // SF // V // VG // P // 749 KJ/179 CAL PER SERVE // SERVES 1

250 ml (9 fl oz/1 cup) water
45 g (1½ oz/1 cup) baby
  spinach leaves
15 g (½ oz/½ cup) kale ribbons
  (stalks removed, leaves
  sliced)
190 g (6½ oz/1 cup) chopped
  pineapple
75 g (2¾ oz/½ cup)
  strawberries
30 g (1 oz/½ cup) coarsely
  chopped broccoli florets
1 small orange
1 thumb-size piece of ginger

Put all the ingredients into a blender and process for about 1 minute until smooth.

NOTE

✳ This is a total immunity boosting smoothie.

You really want the pineapple to be super sweet and ripe for this recipe to balance out the flavour of the beetroot.

TURN UP THE BEET

DF // GF // NF // SF // V // VG // P // 853 KJ/204 CAL PER SERVE // SERVES 1

250 ml (9 fl oz/1 cup) coconut
    water
65 g (2½ oz/1½ cups) baby
    spinach leaves
15 g (½ oz/½ cup) kale ribbons
    (stalks removed, leaves
    sliced)
1 beetroot (beet), peeled and
    chopped
190 g (6½ oz/1 cup) chopped
    pineapple

Put all the ingredients in a blender and blend
until smooth. We garnished ours with edible
flowers (dianthus) and flaked almonds.

MORNING FUEL

DF // GF // SF // V // VG // P // 1389 KJ/332 CAL PER SERVE // SERVES 1

375 ml (13 fl oz/1½ cups)
    coconut water
90 g (3¼ oz/2 cups) baby
    spinach leaves
¼ small avocado
¼ pear
1 red apple, cored
5 almonds

Put all the ingredients into a blender and process
until smooth, then add the toppings of your choice.

We've used:
* millet puffs
* blueberries
* mint
* desiccated (shredded) coconut

POMEGRANATE FLUSH

DF // NF // SF // V // VG // P // 1263 KJ/302 CAL PER SERVE // SERVES 1

90 g (3¼ oz/2 cups) baby
    spinach leaves
15 g (½ oz/¼ cup) broccoli florets
155 g (5½ oz/1 cup) frozen
    blueberries
½ frozen banana
125 ml (4 fl oz/½ cup)
    pomegranate juice
125 ml (4 fl oz/½ cup) water
1 tablespoon cleansing fibre
    powder

Put all the ingredients into a blender and process
until smooth.

NOTE

＊ Cleansing fibre powder can be found in the health-
    food aisle of your supermarket.

PINE-ING FOR YOU

DF // GF // NF // SF // V // VG // P // 1251 KJ/299 CAL PER SERVE // SERVES 1;
MAKES 2 CUPS (500 ML/17 FL OZ)

45 g (1½ oz/1 cup) baby
    spinach leaves
25 g (1 oz/1 cup) kale ribbons
    (stalks removed, leaves
    sliced)
160 g (5¾ oz/½ cup) frozen
    chopped mango
190 g (6½ oz/1 cup) chopped
    pineapple
250 ml (9 fl oz/1 cup) coconut
    water
1 teaspoon coconut oil

Put all the ingredients into a blender and process
until smooth.

pomegranate
flush

pine-ing for you

SUPERCHARGE YOUR SMOOTHIE

YOU CAN ADD TO YOUR SMOOTHIE

* aloe vera juice
* avocado
* chlorophyll
* cacao
* medjool dates
* cleansing fibre powder
* herbs—mint, basil, parsley
* nut butters—almond, macadamia, cacao, peanut
* nuts and seeds—almonds, pistachios, pumpkin seeds (pepitas), sesame seeds, walnuts
* oils—coconut, flaxseed
* powders—acai berry, maca, matcha, probiotic, protein, SWIISH DELIISH Super Green Superfood Powder
* rolled (porridge) oats
* spices—cinnamon, cayenne pepper, ginger, turmeric
* sweeteners— honey, maple syrup, rice malt syrup, stevia
* yoghurts—Greek, coconut, vanilla

SHOW-STOPPING TOPPERS FOR YOUR SMOOTHIES

* avocado slices
* bee pollen
* berries—strawberries, blueberries, raspberries, blackberries; frozen berries also look amazing
* buckwheat (but soak it first!)
* cacao nibs
* coconut—desiccated (shredded) or shaved
* edible flowers
* fruit—banana, dragonfruit balls, fig, kiwi, mango, passionfruit, persimmon, star fruit, pineapple, honeydew melon, rockmelon (cantaloupe)
* goji berries
* grains— granola, puffed millet or puffed quinoa
* herbs—basil, mint, oregano
* lemon or lime zest/wedges
* nuts—flaked almonds, chopped pistachios, chopped hazelnuts
* seeds—pomegranate, chia, sesame, sunflower
* whipped smoothies in another colour (see our recipes on pages 70 and 96)
* yoghurt—your choice, dolloped on top
* cranberries
* craisins

THE ANNIHILATOR

DF // GF // NF // SF // V // VG // P
284 KJ/68 CAL PER SERVE
SERVES 1

1–2 fresh lemons
large knob of fresh ginger
   (about 3–4 cm/1½–2 in)
¼ apple, peeled and cored
1 clove of fresh garlic
2 drops oil of oregano (not oregano oil,
   as the potency is very different)
1 teaspoon raw apple cider vinegar
dash of ground turmeric
dash of ground cayenne pepper

Juice the lemon, ginger, apple and
garlic. Add the oil of oregano, apple
cider vinegar and finally a dash each
of turmeric and cayenne pepper. It's
potent but it works.

DIGESTION BOOSTER SHOT

DF // GF // NF // SF // V // VG // P
84 KJ/20 CAL PER SERVE
SERVES 1

¼ teaspoon ground ginger
2 tablespoons lemon juice
2 tablespoons apple cider vinegar

Mix the ingredients together and drink
immediately.

We call it this because we find it helps annihilate any bug or germ.

E-V-A (ENERGY VITALITY ALKALINE) SUPERFOOD SHOT

DF // GF // NF // SF // V // VG // P
54 KJ/13 CAL PER SERVE
SERVES 1

125 ml (4 fl oz/½ cup) water
1 teaspoon SWIISH DELIISH Super Green
    Superfood Powder
juice of ½ lime

Mix the ingredients together and drink immediately.

ANTI-INFLAMMATORY TURMERIC TONIC

DF // GF // NF // V // VG // P
211 KJ/50 CAL PER SERVE
SERVES 1

250 ml (8½ fl oz/1 cup) coconut water
1 tablespoon grated fresh turmeric (or
    ½ teaspoon dried turmeric powder)
½ tablespoon grated fresh ginger
juice from ½ lemon (or, if you prefer, from
    ½ orange)
½ medium carrot
½ tablespoon maple syrup or honey
pinch of black pepper
pinch of cayenne pepper or cinnamon

Place all the ingredients into a high-speed blender and blend until smooth.

This healing tonic is a great way to reduce inflammation. The turmeric gives your immune system a boost.

— CHAPTER TWO —

salads

EAT THE RAINBOW SALAD

DF // GF // SF // V // VG // P // 933 KJ/223 CAL PER SERVE // SERVES 4

½ cauliflower (approx. 300 g/
   10½ oz)
1 garlic clove
7 g (¼ oz/¼ cup) coriander
   (cilantro) leaves, finely
   chopped
7 g (¼ oz/¼ cup) mint leaves,
   finely chopped
3 spring onions (scallions),
   finely chopped
½ red capsicum (pepper),
   chopped
½ yellow capsicum (pepper),
   chopped
¼ red cabbage, finely sliced
zest of 2 limes (use the juice for
   dressing)
60 ml (2 fl oz/¼ cup)
   unsweetened tinned
   coconut milk
2 mangoes, cubed
40 g (1½ oz/¼ cup) salted
   cashews, halved

DRESSING (OPTIONAL)
2 tablespoons peanut butter
juice of 2 limes
2 tablespoons rice malt syrup
   or honey
60 ml (2 fl oz/¼ cup) water
1 fresh red chilli (optional)

Using a food processor, pulse the cauliflower and garlic until it becomes like 'rice', then put it in a microwave-safe dish with 2 tablespoons water and cover with plastic wrap. Microwave for 3 minutes.

While the cauliflower 'rice' is cooking, put the coriander, mint and spring onion in a bowl with the red and yellow capsicum, cabbage and lime zest.

When the cauliflower 'rice' is cooked, stir in the coconut milk and add it to the bowl with the vegetables.

Whisk together the dressing ingredients and drizzle it over the salad.

Toss the mango through the salad. This is best done by hand so as to keep the mango intact. Top with cashews and serve.

NOTE
* We do all the chopping for this salad in a food processor. It just makes it so much easier and quicker!

SMOKED TROUT AND MANGO SALAD

DF // GF // NF // SF // P // 1356 KJ/324 CAL PER SERVE // SERVES 2

90 g (3¼ oz/2 cups) baby
    spinach leaves
200 g (7 oz) hot smoked
    trout, sliced
1 large mango, thinly sliced
115 g (4 oz/1 cup) bean sprouts
2 spring onions (scallions),
    thinly sliced
1 fresh red or green chilli,
    seeded and thinly sliced
15 g (½ oz/½ cup) mint leaves,
    roughly torn
15 g (½ oz/½ cup) coriander
    (cilantro) leaves, roughly
    torn

DRESSING (OPTIONAL)

1 garlic clove
2 tablespoons lime juice
2 tablespoons fish sauce
2 tablespoons rice malt syrup
2 tablespoons coriander
    (cilantro) leaves, finely
    chopped
1 fresh red chilli, seeded and
    finely chopped

In a small bowl, mix together all the ingredients for
the dressing.

On a platter, place the baby spinach leaves. Top
with the trout, mango slices, sprouts, spring onion,
chilli and herbs.

Spoon the dressing generously over the top
and serve.

NOTES

✳ This salad also works really well with tinned tuna.
   We suggest using tuna in spring water; because the
   dressing is so flavoursome, it's best to use tuna that
   is closer to its natural flavour.

✳ You can get smoked trout at the supermarket.
   It comes shrink-wrapped and in a fillet. Here we've
   used hot smoked river trout, but you can also use
   rainbow trout, or even hot smoked salmon. They all
   work beautifully in this recipe.

MAPLE MISO PUMPKIN WITH SOBA NOODLE

DF // NF // SF // V // VG // 1858 KJ/444 CAL PER SERVE // SERVES 2
1238 KJ/296 CAL PER SERVE // SERVES 3

400 g (14 oz) butternut
   pumpkin, sliced
100 g (3½ oz) dried soba
   noodles
155 g (5½ oz/1 cup) frozen
   whole edamame (or shelled
   beans if you can find them
   at Asian grocers)
300 g (10½ oz) sugar snap
   peas or snow peas
   (mangetout)
300 g (10½ oz) green beans
100 g (3½ oz) broccolini
2 fresh red chillies, thinly sliced
   (optional)

PUMPKIN MARINADE
AND NOODLE DRESSING
(OPTIONAL)
2 tablespoons sesame oil
2 tablespoons maple syrup
2 tablespoons sesame seeds
2 teaspoons miso paste

Preheat the oven to 180°C (350°F). Line a baking tray with baking paper.

Mix all the ingredients for the marinade and dressing together. Divide mixture into two equal portions and set one quantity aside to use as the dressing. Use the other quantity as a marinade to coat the pumpkin. Place the pumpkin slices on the prepared baking tray and roast for about 15 minutes or until cooked through.

While the pumpkin cooks, bring some water to the boil. Put the soba noodles in a heatproof bowl and cover them with boiling water. (Tip: cover the bowl with a plate to trap the heat and help the noodles cook quicker.) It takes about 5 minutes for the noodles to be soft and ready.

In a separate heatproof bowl, cover the edamame with boiling water too. Allow a minute or two to soften, then shell the edamame. Reserve the pods.

Drain the noodles and refresh twice under cold water.

Steam the sugar snap peas, green beans and broccolini in the microwave for about 4–5 minutes until tender.

Using the reserved dressing, toss the noodles with the dressing, then serve with edamame, sugar snap peas, green beans, broccolini and pumpkin. Top with sliced chilli (if using).

ASIAN KAZOODLE SALAD

DF // GF // NF // SF // V // VG // P // 1117 KJ/267 CAL PER SERVE // SERVES 2

2 large zucchini (courgettes),
    spiralised
1 large carrot, spiralised
150 g (5½ oz/2 cups) red
    cabbage, shredded
50 g (1¾ oz/2 cups) kale
    ribbons, massaged
1 red capsicum (pepper), thinly
    sliced
1 yellow capsicum (pepper),
    thinly sliced
3 tablespoons chia seeds
    (black and white)

DRESSING (OPTIONAL)

2 teaspoons fish sauce
2 tablespoons soy sauce
80 ml (2½ fl oz/⅓ cup) lime
    juice
1 tablespoon rice malt syrup
2 teaspoons sesame seeds

Put all the salad ingredients into a large bowl.

Make the dressing by combining all the ingredients in a small jar and shaking well.

Pour the dressing over the salad, and toss to ensure the salad is well coated. Serve immediately and enjoy.

NOTE

＊ How do you massage kale? *Glad you asked!* Simply take the leaves once they've been chopped or sliced and use your hands to rub the kale (as if you're massaging it) until it begins to soften. You can use a little olive oil or coconut oil if you like. This process basically makes the kale easier to eat as it breaks down the toughness of the leaf and also removes some of the bitterness.

THE FIVE-MINUTE SATISFIER

DF // GF // NF // SF // V // VG // 1598 KJ/382 CAL PER SERVE // SERVES 2

250 g (9 oz) packet 90-second microwave brown rice & quinoa

2 spring onions (scallions), finely chopped

¼ red cabbage, finely chopped

120 g (4¼ oz/2 cups) coarsely chopped broccoli, including stems

15 g (½ oz/½ cup) coriander (cilantro) leaves, finely chopped

15 g (½ oz/½ cup) basil leaves, finely chopped

10 g (⅜ oz/½ cup) mint leaves, finely chopped

40 g (1½ oz/¼ cup) sesame seeds, lightly toasted

zest of 2 limes, juice reserved for the dressing

DRESSING (OPTIONAL)

juice of 2 limes

1 tablespoon fish sauce

1 teaspoon crushed fresh ginger

1 tablespoon olive oil

1 teaspoon sesame oil

Cook the brown rice & quinoa in the microwave according to the packet instructions.

Combine all the vegetables and herbs with the sesame seeds in a bowl.

Add the lime zest to the salad (reserve the lime juice for the dressing!).

Mix all the dressing ingredients together and set aside.

Add the brown rice & quinoa to the vegetable mixture and mix well.

If serving immediately, add the dressing and stir through. If you are preparing this salad ahead of time, keep the dressing separate until you are ready to eat.

I call this my food-processor salad so if you have one, now is the time to dust it off and use it. Honestly, this salad takes about 5 minutes to make.

– SALLY

PUMPKIN AND MACADAMIA QUINOA CROWD PLEASER

DF // GF // SF // V // VG // P // 2498 KJ/597 CAL PER SERVE // SERVES 2

*400 g (14 oz) butternut
pumpkin, cubed*
1 tablespoon olive oil
*pink salt and freshly ground
black pepper*
*250 g (9 oz) packet 90-second
microwave brown rice &
quinoa*
*60 g (2 oz/1 cup) flat-leaf
(Italian) parsley, finely
chopped*
*½ red (Spanish) onion, finely
chopped*
*30 g (1 oz/¼ cup) macadamia
nuts, halved*
*40 g (1½ oz/¼ cup) sweetened
dried cranberries*

DRESSING (OPTIONAL)
2 tablespoons olive oil
1 tablespoon maple syrup

Preheat the oven to 180°C (350°F). Line a baking tray with baking paper. Coat the cubed pumpkin with the olive oil and season with salt and pepper. Bake for 25 minutes or until cooked through.

Cook the brown rice & quinoa in the microwave, following the packet instructions.

Combine the parsley, onion, macadamia nuts and cranberries in a bowl. Add the brown rice & quinoa and mix well.

Add the pumpkin and stir to combine.

Whisk the olive oil and maple syrup together and drizzle over the salad.

TIPS

* *To save time,* you can buy your pumpkin peeled and cubed.

* If you would like your salad to have extra crunch or sweetness, just add more macadamias and cranberries.

THE DEBRIEF SALAD

NF // SF // VG // 2102 KJ/502 CAL PER SERVE // SERVES 6

250 g (9 oz) pearl (big)
    couscous
pink salt and freshly ground
    black pepper
250 g (9 oz) packet 90-second
    microwave red quinoa
400 g (14 oz) tin brown lentils
50 g (1¾ oz/1 cup) finely sliced
    mint leaves
zest and juice of 2 lemons
2 red (Spanish) onions, finely
    chopped
4 spring onions (scallions),
    sliced
seeds of 1 pomegranate
60 ml (2 fl oz/¼ cup) olive oil
150 g (5½ oz) feta cheese,
    crumbled

Put the pearl couscous in a saucepan and cover with 625 ml (21½ fl oz/2½ cups) of water. Season generously with salt and pepper. Cover and simmer for 8–10 minutes, stirring occasionally.

While that cooks, microwave the red quinoa following the packet instructions.

Drain the lentils and rinse under cold running water. Leave to drain completely.

Put the mint, lemon zest, onion, spring onion and pomegranate seeds in a bowl. Add the drained couscous, quinoa and lentils to the bowl and mix well.

Add the olive oil and lemon juice to the salad and mix well. Serve topped with crumbled feta.

TIPS

✳ If you can't get pomegranates, simply replace the seeds with sweetened dried cranberries. They taste just as amazing in this recipe.

✳ Quinoa—like meat, chicken or fish—is a full-chain protein, so it's a perfect substitute for meats.

✳ *We call this The Debrief Salad* because this is what we make for ourselves and our friends when we need to debrief and download—whether it's work, men, or life in general. This salad is substantial and hearty, and ensures that a group of gabbling girls can talk and talk and talk for hours!

We like to use Persian or Danish feta, as the taste is smoother and the consistency is softer.

LENTIL AS ANYTHING SALAD

DF // GF // NF // SF // VG // 1820 KJ/435 CAL PER SERVE // SERVES 3

250 g (9 oz) packet 90-second
  microwave brown rice
400 g (14 oz) tin brown lentils
2 Lebanese (short) cucumbers
1 large or 2 small zucchini
  (courgettes)
1 green capsicum (pepper)
45 g (1½ oz/1 cup) baby
  spinach leaves, roughly
  chopped
25 g (1 oz/½ cup) roughly
  chopped mint leaves
2 tablespoons olive oil
pink salt and freshly ground
  black pepper

DRESSING (OPTIONAL)
260 g (9¼ oz/1 cup) Greek-
  style yoghurt
1 small garlic clove, crushed
1 tablespoon chopped mint
1 tablespoon chopped dill
1 green chilli, thinly sliced
  (optional)
pink salt and freshly ground
  black pepper

Cook the brown rice in the microwave according
to packet instructions.

Drain and wash the lentils a few times and set aside
to drain.

Finely chop the cucumber, zucchini, capsicum, baby
spinach and mint. Combine these together in a bowl.

Add the brown rice and lentils to the salad bowl
and mix well with the olive oil. Season with salt
and pepper.

Mix the dressing ingredients together with a
generous grind of salt and pepper and drizzle over
the salad.

MYKONOS SUMMER NIGHT'S SALAD

DF // GF // NF // SF // VG // 1351 KJ/323 CAL PER SERVE // SERVES 2

450 g (16 oz/3 cups) cherry or
  grape tomatoes, halved
2 zucchini (courgettes), sliced
  into thin ribbons
½ red (Spanish) onion,
  chopped
80 g (3 oz/½ cup) tinned
  chickpeas, rinsed and
  drained
2 Lebanese (short) cucumbers,
  chopped (leave the skin on,
  for colour and fibre, just
  make sure you wash it well)
3 tablespoons chopped dill
3 teaspoons chopped oregano
130 g (4½ oz/1 cup) crumbled
  Greek feta cheese
zest of 1 lemon
75 g (2¾ oz/½ cup) pitted
  kalamata olives
pink salt and freshly ground
  black pepper

DRESSING (OPTIONAL)
juice of ½ a lemon
60 ml (2 fl oz/¼ cup) olive oil
1 tablespoon oregano, dried or
  fresh
3 teaspoons rice malt syrup
½ teaspoon crushed garlic
70 g (2½ oz/¼ cup) Greek-
  style yoghurt
pink salt and freshly ground
  black pepper

Toss together all the salad ingredients in a serving bowl. Season with pink salt and freshly ground black pepper to taste.

Mix the dressing (if using) in a small bowl or jar and season with pink salt and freshly ground black pepper.

NOTE

✳ We sometimes like to do a mix of whole, halved, quartered and sliced vegetables, just for variety.

I eat my salad as is, with only a drizzle of olive oil —as I would if I were on holidays in Greece.

– SALLY

I love mine with the dressing. For me, the yoghurt takes things up a notch.

– MAHA

TOTALLY SUBLIME VERMICELLI SALAD

DF // GF // NF // V // VG // P // 1351 KJ/323 CAL PER SERVE // SERVES 2

125 g (4½ oz) vermicelli rice
    noodles
1 carrot, thinly sliced
⅛ red cabbage, thinly sliced
⅛ green cabbage, thinly sliced
15 g (½ oz/½ cup) kale ribbons
    (stalks removed, leaves
    sliced)
1 Lebanese (short) cucumber,
    sliced
½ red capsicum (pepper),
    sliced
1 spring onion (scallion), sliced
5 g (⅛ oz/¼ cup) mint leaves,
    shredded
7 g (¼ oz/¼ cup) coriander
    (cilantro) leaves, shredded
grated zest of 1 lime, juice
    reserved for the dressing

DRESSING (OPTIONAL)

80 ml (2½ fl oz/⅓ cup) soy
    sauce
2 tablespoons maple syrup
juice of 1 lime
1 tablespoon olive oil
1 tablespoon sesame oil
1 small garlic clove, grated
1 tablespoon chilli paste

Put the noodles into a heatproof bowl and cover
with boiling water. Stand for about 3 minutes until
softened.

Mix all the dressing ingredients together. Adjust the
amount of chilli paste to suit your taste, if necessary.

Drain and refresh the noodles under cold running
water. Put them in a bowl with the remaining
ingredients and toss them all together.

Slowly add the dressing to taste and serve.

NOTES

* This is better mixed by hand so that you can ensure
  the noodles are well separated and the lime zest is
  dispersed.

* If you aren't eating this salad immediately, drizzle a
  little olive oil over the noodles so they don't clump
  tougher. Give them a good mix to ensure they are
  well coated, then toss through the salad.

* If you wanted to amp up this salad you could add
  shredded barbecued chicken or grilled pork fillets.

* Leftover dressing can be refrigerated and used for
  up to 2 weeks.

FRESH PRAWN AND PAPAYA SALAD

DF // GF // NF // SF // P // 1661 KJ/397 CAL PER SERVE // SERVES 2

1 ripe papaya
1 firm avocado
½ red (Spanish) onion
1 red chilli, seeded (optional)
20 g (¾ oz/¼ cup) finely
    chopped basil leaves
25 g (1 oz/¼ cup) finely
    chopped coriander
    (cilantro) leaves
25 g (1 oz/¼ cup) finely
    chopped mint leaves
20 cooked king prawns
    (shrimp), then peeled
    and deveined

DRESSING (OPTIONAL)
juice of 1 lime, zest reserved
juice of 1 lemon
1 teaspoon pink salt
freshly ground black pepper

Make the dressing first. Squeeze the lime and lemon juice into a large bowl, then add the salt and pepper and mix well.

Peel and deseed the papaya and chop into small cubes. Add to the bowl with the dressing.

Chop the avocado into small cubes and add to the papaya and dressing.

Finely chop the onion and red chilli (if using) and add to the papaya and avocado mixture in the bowl.

Add the herbs to the bowl, then add the lime zest and mix well.

To serve, place the prawns on top of the salad and season with a little salt and pepper.

NOTE

* When we make this for a lunch on the go or for a picnic, we peel and devein the prawns and then chop the flesh and mix it through the salad. It's so delicious because the prawn soaks up all the flavour of the dressing. But if I'm making this salad at home I serve the prawns on the side and let everyone do it for themselves! – SALLY

BEET IT SALAD

GF // NF // SF // VG // 1699 KJ/406 CAL PER SERVE // SERVES 4

SALAD
155 g (5½ oz/1 cup) frozen
    whole edamame (or shelled
    beans if you can find them
    at Asian grocers)
100 g (3½ oz/4 cups) kale
    ribbons (stalks removed,
    leaves sliced), massaged
4 beetroots (beet)
40 g (1½ oz/¼ cup) pumpkin
    seeds (pepitas)
40 g (1½ oz/¼ cup) sunflower
    seeds
4 radishes, sliced
100 g (3½ oz) goat's cheese,
    crumbled
1 tablespoon olive oil, for
    massaging the kale
1 tablespoon mint leaves, thinly
    sliced
1 tablespoon black and white
    chia seeds

DRESSING (OPTIONAL)
60 ml (2 fl oz/¼ cup) apple
    cider vinegar
2 tablespoons lime juice
2 tablespoons olive oil
15 g (½ oz/¼ cup) chopped
    mint leaves
2 tablespoons rice malt syrup
½–1 teaspoon dijon mustard, to
    taste
pink salt and freshly ground
    black pepper

Cook the edamame by bringing water to the boil and pouring it over the beans in a heatproof bowl, blanching them for about 2 minutes. Drain and allow to cool, then remove the beans from the pods. Combine the edamame and the kale in a bowl.

Peel the beetroot, leaving the tail on. Shred the beetroot, using a grater, mandolin or a food processor. We personally find that the grater is easy and doesn't get stained crimson!

To prepare the dressing, whisk together all the ingredients. Season with salt and pepper.

To assemble the salad in a serving bowl, put the beetroot in first, then add the kale and edamame. Add the pumpkin seeds (pepitas) and sunflower seeds next. Add the dressing and gently toss to combine. Then add the sliced radish, goat's cheese and mint leaves (add these last so they don't turn pink). Finally, sprinkle with the chia seeds and serve.

NOTE
* Before massaging the kale, see page 127.

TIPS
* When preparing the beetroot, use gloves to avoid staining your hands and nails. Peel the beetroot but leave the tail on: this gives you something to hold onto when you're grating.

* To bulk this up, add a can of red kidney beans or a couple of soft-boiled eggs—delicious with this salad!

MAPLE SPROUT AND KALE SALAD

DF // GF // SF // V // VG // P // 912 KJ/218 CAL PER SERVE // SERVES 2
456 KJ/109 CAL PER SERVE // SERVES 4

500 g (1 lb 2 oz) Brussels
    sprouts
50 g (1¾ oz/2 cups) kale
    ribbons (stalks removed,
    leaves sliced)
72 g (2½ oz/½ cup) sweetened
    dried cranberries
70 g (2½ oz/½ cup) chopped
    brazil nuts

DRESSING (OPTIONAL)
80 ml (2½ fl oz/⅓ cup) olive oil
2 tablespoons white wine
    vinegar
2 teaspoons dijon mustard
1 teaspoon maple syrup
pink salt and freshly ground
    black pepper

Thinly slice the Brussels sprouts. Steam half the
Brussels sprouts in a microwave with 60 ml (2 fl oz/
¼ cup) of water for about 2–3 minutes until soft.

In a bowl, combine the kale and the remaining
uncooked Brussels sprouts, then add the cranberries
and the brazil nuts.

Mix together the dressing ingredients in a bowl,
season with salt and freshly ground black pepper
and whisk until combined.

When the Brussels sprouts have finished cooking,
drain the water and add them to the salad. Add the
dressing and toss to mix well.

NOTES

* The mix of the raw and cooked Brussels sprouts
  provides a variety of flavours and textures.

* Instead of the cranberries you can use pomegranate
  when it's in season, as it works really well with the
  Brussels sprouts and kale.

To round this out as a meal, add grilled chicken. It's also perfect with white fish.

YOU, ME AND CAPRI SALAD

GF // NF // SF // P // 1770 KJ/423 CAL PER SERVE // SERVES 2

2 Lebanese (short) cucumbers,
    chopped
2 roma (plum) tomatoes,
    chopped
1 zucchini (courgette), chopped
½ red capsicum (pepper),
    chopped
15 g (½ oz/¼ cup) finely
    chopped spring onions
    (scallions)
7 g (¼ oz/¼ cup) chopped
    mint leaves
¼ red (Spanish) onion,
    chopped
60 g (2¼ oz/½ cup) black
    olives, halved
200 g (7 oz/1 cup) ready-
    made roasted red capsicum
    (peppers), sliced
270 g (9½ oz) tinned
    artichokes
    in brine
120 g (4¼ oz) goat's cheese
50 g (1¾ oz) white anchovies

DRESSING (OPTIONAL)
juice of ½ lemon
2 tablespoons olive oil
1 teaspoon crushed garlic
pink salt and freshly ground
    black pepper, to season

Mix the dressing ingredients together in a small bowl. Add the salad ingredients and toss to combine. Top with feta and white anchovies.

TIP

✳ This salad goes so well with grilled fish, tinned tuna or even barbecued chicken (just leave out the anchovies). For vegetarians it goes really well with cannellini beans.

SUPER POWER SALAD

DF // GF // SF // NF // VG // P // 1816 KJ/434 CAL PER SERVE // SERVES 2

90 g (3 oz/1 cup) chopped
　　broccolini
100 g (3½ oz/1 cup) snow peas
　　(mangetout)
2 kale leaves, stalks removed
　　and leaves massaged and
　　shredded
1 zucchini (courgette),
　　spiralised
1 avocado, halved and sliced
1 Lebanese (short) cucumber,
　　halved and sliced
150 g (5½ oz/1 cup) yellow and
　　red cherry tomatoes, halved
4 radishes, sliced
1 carrot, grated
1 beetroot (beet), grated
1 tablespoon olive oil, for
　　massaging the kale
2 hard-boiled eggs, halved

DRESSING (OPTIONAL)
80 ml (2½ fl oz/⅓ cup) olive oil
2 tablespoons lemon juice
1 tablespoon finely grated
　　lemon zest
1 tablespoon rice malt syrup
1 tablespoon chia seeds
pink salt and freshly ground
　　black pepper

Cook the broccolini in the microwave for about
3 minutes or until soft. Cook the snow peas in the
microwave for about 2 minutes or until soft.

Mix all the dressing ingredients together. Season
with salt and pepper and whisk to combine.

Combine all the vegetables on serving plates, top
with the eggs and serve with dressing on the side.

NOTES

✳ When you grate the beetroot, use plastic gloves so
you don't stain your hands. When we don't have
plastic gloves handy we improvise by using freezer
bags on our hands ... it's just as effective!

✳ *We use a combination of both* black and
white chia seeds, but either is fine.

✳ We explain how to massage kale on page 127.

— CHAPTER THREE —

bowls

BOWLS

Yep, bowls. Aren't they something you put your food into, you ask? Well, yes. But they're so much more than that these days.

Smoothie bowls, chia bowls, breakfast bowls, Buddha bowls, nourishing bowls, macro bowls, quinoa bowls ... the list goes on, and so it should. Bowls are taking the world by storm. This isn't just a passing fad, bowls are here to stay: they're a way of eating a whole rainbow of deliciously nutritious, satisfying ingredients without overdoing it. They look and taste amazing, plus they're soooo good for you!

So, what's a bowl made of? Well, each one is typically a combo of greens, grains, veggies and protein, amped up with special additions here and there, such as fermented foods, special sauces (think tahini sauce) and plentiful toppings.

It's no wonder that homewares companies are reporting massive increases in the sale of bowls! We love that, because it means that more and more people are choosing to embrace eating this way.

Although we have a whole heap of incredibly tasty and healthy bowl recipes for you to follow, we also want to help you create your own combinations because, well, it's fun to experiment and play, and you get to use the ingredients you have in your pantry and fridge, meaning that there is less waste (love that!).

Just follow our guide on pages 156–7.

Bowls are everywhere. Walk into any cafe, scroll through anyone's social media feed, read any magazine: bowls are where it's at. What's the big deal? you might be asking. Doesn't anyone eat on a plate anymore? Apparently not.

Our mum used to do 'bowls' when we were growing up, only she called them 'leftover parties' in an attempt to make us more excited about the fact that she was basically rustling up a meal from bits and pieces in the fridge, pantry and veggie drawer.

She was spot-on though; it was a mix of vegetables, grains, protein, heathy fats and almost always some kind of delicious dressing that brought the whole thing together. She was clearly two decades ahead of the trend, but it's no wonder bowls are taking over the food-sphere.

HOW TO BUILD A BOWL

Want to build your own bowl? Here's a little guide to help you get it right.

1. START WITH VEGGIES

* beetroot (beet)
* cabbage—green, red
* capsicum (pepper)
* carrots
* cauliflower
* tomatoes
* lettuce
* cucumber
* snow peas (mangetout)

Load up on the veggies—they create the framework.

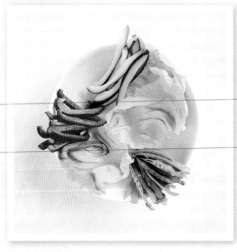

2. ADD THE GRAINS OR LOW-GI CARBS

* couscous
* freekeh
* legumes—chickpeas, butter beans, borlotti beans, kidney beans, lentils
* noodles—soba, vermicelli
* rice—black, brown
* veggies—corn, sweet potato

This should take up roughly a quarter of the bowl.

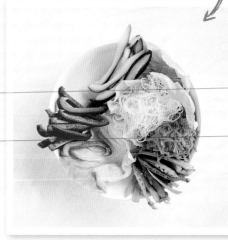

3. ADD THE PROTEIN

* chicken
* eggs
* fish—salmon, tinned sardines, tuna
* quinoa
* red meat
* tofu

Another quarter of the bowl.

4. ADD GOOD FATS + FLAVOUR

* avocado
* nuts—almonds, cashews, hazelnuts, pistachios
* oils—coconut, olive
* seeds—chia, sesame
* tahini
* mango

5. ADD THE TOPPINGS

* feta cheese—Danish, Greek, Persian
* berries—cranberries, goji
* herbs—coriander (cilantro), mint, oregano, parsley—and sprouts
* hummus
* olives
* pickled veggies—kimchi, sauerkraut
* roasted red capsicum (pepper)
* seeds—pumpkin (pepitas), sunflower, pomegranate
* yoghurt
* chilli

Don't forget the toppings—they really elevate the flavours!

COCONUT CHIA BOWL

DF // GF // NF // SF // V // VG // P // 1232 KJ/294 CAL PER SERVE // SERVES 2

250 ml (9 fl oz/1 cup)
   unsweetened coconut milk
   (carton variety)
2 tablespoons desiccated
   (shredded) coconut
3 tablespoons chia seeds
2 teaspoons stevia

Put the ingredients in a mixing bowl and stir well to combine. Cover with plastic wrap and leave to set in the fridge overnight.

The toppings are totally up to you: you can top your bowl with whatever you feel like!

We've used:
* kiwifruit
* mango
* passionfruit
* strawberries
* blueberries
* desiccated (shredded) coconut
* cacao nibs

TIP

* Some carton-variety coconut milks are made up of different ingredients (such as a combination of coconut milk and almond milk, or coconut milk and rice milk, or even coconut milk and water). So, if you find your chia pudding is still runny even after it's been in the fridge overnight, add an extra tablespoon of chia seeds to help absorb the extra liquid. Stir and return to the fridge for a few more hours to set.

QUINOA BREKKIE BOWL

DF // GF // NF // SF // V // VG // P // 1573 KJ/376 CAL PER SERVE // SERVES 2

75 g (2½ oz/½ cup) quinoa
125 ml (4 fl oz/½ cup)
   unsweetened coconut milk
   (carton variety)
4 medjool dates, seeded and
   roughly chopped
1 teaspoon ground cinnamon
pinch of nutmeg
pinch of ground cardamon
2 teaspoons sunflower seeds
2 tablespoons moist coconut
   flakes, plus extra for serving
   (optional)
1 x 125 g (4½ oz) punnet
   blueberries
1 x 250 g (9 oz) punnet
   strawberries

Rinse the quinoa under cold water until the water runs clear (make sure the holes in your sieve aren't bigger than the quinoa—Maha learnt this the hard way!).

Put the quinoa into a saucepan with 375 ml (13 fl oz/1½ cups) of water, the coconut milk and the chopped dates. Bring the mixture to the boil, then reduce the heat to simmer for 15–20 minutes, stirring occasionally and making sure that the quinoa doesn't stick to the bottom of the saucepan.

Once the quinoa has begun to soften, add the spices, sunflower seeds and coconut flakes. Continue to cook for another 5–10 minutes, until the quinoa has cooked.

Serve immediately. We topped ours with fresh berries, extra coconut flakes, goji berries, pumpkin seeds (pepitas) and Greek-style yoghurt.

TIP
* For extra sweetness, drizzle with a little honey or rice malt syrup.

I love a good dollop of Greek-style yoghurt on mine!
– MAHA

MISS SAIGON BRUSSELS SPROUTS BOWL

DF // GF // NF // SF // P // 1310 KJ/313 CAL PER SERVE // SERVES 2

4 pancetta or bacon strips
    (about 70 g/2½ oz)
500 g (1 lb 2 oz) Brussels
    sprouts
2 eggs
2 teaspoons olive oil, for frying
120 g (4¼ oz/1 cup) spring
    onions (scallions), sliced
1 fresh red chilli, thinly sliced
    (optional)

DRESSING (OPTIONAL)
80 ml (2½ fl oz/⅓ cup) soy
    sauce
2 teaspoons crushed garlic
1 teaspoon grated fresh ginger
80 ml (2¾ fl oz/⅓ cup) rice
    malt syrup
¼ teaspoon fish sauce

Fry the pancetta or bacon until crispy. Chop into small pieces and set aside.

Finely slice the Brussels sprouts. Put them in a large bowl, add 60 ml (2 fl oz/¼ cup) of water and microwave on High for 2–3 minutes or until soft.

Make the dressing by whisking all the ingredients together in a bowl.

Fry the eggs in a small non-stick frying pan with a dash of olive oil. If you prefer cooked spring onion then you can also cook them at this point, to bring out their flavour.

To serve, divide the Brussels sprouts and spring onion between two serving bowls, top with a quarter of the dressing. Crumble over the pancetta. Place the egg on top and drizzle with the remainder of the dressing.

Top with the chilli (if using).

SANTORINI SALMON BOWL

GF // NF // SF // P // 1824 KJ/436 CAL PER SERVE // SERVES 2

2 x 150 g (5½ oz) salmon fillets
1 teaspoon olive oil

MARINADE
1 teaspoon olive oil
60 ml (2 fl oz/¼ cup) lemon
    juice
½ tablespoon flat-leaf (Italian)
    parsley, finely chopped
1 tablespoon oregano, finely
    chopped
1 garlic clove, crushed
1 teaspoon smoked paprika
1 tablespoon caramelised
    balsamic vinegar

SALAD BOWL
1 red capsicum (pepper), seeded
    and sliced
150 g (5¼ oz/1 cup) sweet red
    cherry tomatoes, halved
1 Lebanese (short) cucumber,
    quartered
12 kalamata olives (optional)
120 g (4¼ oz) Greek feta cheese,
    cubed (optional)
¼ red (Spanish) onion, sliced
1 teaspoon olive oil (optional)
squeeze of lemon juice, to taste
pink salt and freshly ground
    black pepper

Combine the marinade ingredients in a medium-size bowl. Add the salmon fillets to the bowl and coat with the marinade, ensuring that both pieces are thoroughly covered. Leave the salmon to marinate for about 15–20 minutes.

While the salmon is marinating, make tzatziki (if using) by combining all the ingredients in a small bowl or jar and seasoning with salt and pepper.

Next, arrange the salad ingredients in two bowls. Drizzle with olive oil and lemon juice, if desired.

Heat one teaspoon of olive oil in a non-stick frying pan over medium–high heat. Fry the salmon fillets for about 4 minutes on each side or until cooked to your liking.

Place the salmon fillets on top of each salad bowl and serve immediately. We love a good dollop of the tzatziki on top of the salmon.

TZATZIKI DRESSING (OPTIONAL)
✳ 130 g (4½ oz/½ cup) Greek-style yoghurt; zest and juice of ½ lemon; ½ garlic clove, crushed; 1½ tablespoons finely sliced mint leaves; pink salt and freshly ground black pepper

This tzatziki dressing is optional, but it really takes this dish to another level!

NOURISHING ROAST VEGGIE BOWL

DF // NF // SF // V // VG // P // 2272 KJ/543 CAL PER SERVE // SERVES 4

1 medium sweet potato, sliced
2 red (Spanish) onions,
    quartered
1 zucchini (courgette), sliced
125 g (4½ oz/1 cup) cauliflower
    florets
1 red capsicum (pepper),
    seeded and quartered
1 yellow capsicum (pepper),
    seeded and quartered
400 g (14 oz) tin chickpeas
100 g (3½ oz) microwave
    couscous
10 green olives, pitted

VEGETABLE MARINADE
4 tablespoons ready-made
    harissa paste
80 ml (2½ fl oz/⅓ cup) red
    wine vinegar
80 ml (2½ fl oz/⅓ cup) olive oil

CHICKPEA MARINADE
1 teaspoon pink salt
1 teaspoon black pepper
1 teaspoon ground cumin
2 teaspoons smoked paprika

DRESSING (OPTIONAL)
135 g (4¾ oz/½ cup) tahini
125 ml (4 fl oz/½ cup) water
1 lemon, juiced
½ teaspoon chilli flakes
    (optional)

Preheat the oven to 200°C (400°F). Line a baking tray with baking paper.

To make the vegetable marinade, mix together the harissa paste, red wine vinegar and olive oil in a bowl. Add the sweet potato, onion, zucchini, cauliflower and capsicums to the marinade and ensure they are well coated. Spread the vegetables on the prepared tray and roast for 35 minutes.

While the veggies are roasting, drain and rinse the chickpeas. Mix the chickpeas with the ingredients for the chickpea marinade and add them to the oven when there's about 20 minutes left for the veggies.

Cook the couscous in the microwave according to the packet instructions.

Make the dressing by combining all the ingredients in a small bowl or jar.

Divide the couscous and veggies between two serving bowls and add 5 green olives to each bowl. Drizzle the dressing over and enjoy.

NOTES

✳ I like to take the skin off the chickpeas—I personally think it tastes better. The easiest way to do this is to give them a good rub as you rinse them. It takes a few minutes to pick the skins out but it's worth it!
– SALLY

✳ I can't be bothered, so I leave them on! – MAHA

SWEET POTATO NOODLES

GF // SF // VG // 1954 KJ/467 CAL PER SERVE // SERVES 2

155 g (5½ oz/1 cup) cashews
1 teaspoon salt
1 garlic clove (note: this is very
    garlicky, so use half if you
    like)
1 tablespoon olive oil
2 small sweet potatoes,
    spiralised
90 g (3¼ oz/2 cups) firmly
    packed baby spinach
    leaves
4 heaped tablespoons
    crumbled feta cheese
    (optional)
handful of basil leaves

Cover the cashews with water in a bowl and leave to soak for 2–4 hours (or overnight is OK too).

Drain and rinse the cashews thoroughly. Transfer them to a blender and add 185 ml (6 fl oz/¾ cup) of water, salt and garlic. Purée until smooth.

Heat the olive oil in a large non-stick frying pan over medium–high heat and add the sweet potato. Toss until it begins to soften slightly. Then add the baby spinach, about half a cup of cashew purée and half of the feta. Mix well.

Once the sweet potato has cooked, remove from the pan and scatter with the remaining feta, if using. Serve immediately and enjoy!

NOTE
* *Any leftover cashew purée* will keep in the fridge for a couple of days.

We first tried poke (pronounced 'po-kay') on a trip we took to Hawaii with our mum several years ago. Poke is a traditional Hawaiian seafood dish. Think small, bite-size pieces of sashimi in a delicious marinade, served up alongside all kinds of other fresh, mouth-watering ingredients. It's no wonder we became obsessed with creating our own version after we got home. ▷—♡→ *It's super simple to make, and super delicious!*

IT'S ALL POKE BOWL

DF // NF // SF // 2117 KJ/506 CAL PER SERVE // SERVES 1

100 g (3½ oz) sashimi-grade
   tuna, cut into 1 cm (⅜ inch)
   cubes
1 tablespoon spring onions
   (scallions), sliced
½ Lebanese (short) cucumber,
   cut into 1 cm (⅜ inch) cubes
125 g (4½ oz) 40-second
   microwave brown rice
½ small avocado, cut into 1 cm
   (⅜ inch) cubes
40 g (1½ oz/½ cup) shredded
   red cabbage
2 tablespoons red (Spanish)
   onion, finely sliced
7 g (¼ oz/¼ cup) coriander
   (cilantro) leaves, chopped
½ fresh long green chilli,
   seeded and sliced
2 tablespoons pickled ginger

DRESSING (OPTIONAL)
2 tablespoons soy sauce
½ tablespoon sesame seeds
1 teaspoon lemon juice
1 teaspoon sesame oil
1 teaspoon rice vinegar
½ teaspoon dried chilli flakes
½ teaspoon pink salt

In a small bowl, combine the tuna, spring onion
and cucumber. Add the dressing ingredients and
mix together well.

Microwave the rice according to the packet
instructions.

Assemble the bowl by placing the rice on the bottom
and arranging the other ingredients on top. We like to
make sure we get a bit of everything on our fork, or
mix it all together—it's up to you!

SESAME CHICKEN WITH ASIAN CABBAGE SLAW

DF // NF // 2159 KJ/516 CAL PER SERVE // SERVES 4

1 tablespoon olive oil
8 small boneless, skinless
    chicken thighs, halved
    and fat trimmed
pink salt and freshly ground
    black pepper
2 tablespoons spring onions
    (scallions), thinly sliced
2 tablespoons coriander
    (cilantro) leaves
½ fresh long red chilli, seeded
    and thinly sliced (optional)

MARINADE
1½ tablespoons sesame oil
1 tablespoon rice wine vinegar
1 garlic clove, crushed
2 tablespoons tahini
½ tablespoon rice malt syrup
1½ tablespoons water
1 tablespoon soy sauce

CABBAGE SLAW
90 g (3¼ oz/2 cups) shredded
    Chinese cabbage (wombok)
150 g (5½ oz/2 cups) shredded
    red cabbage
2 carrots, grated
1 spring onion (scallion), thinly
    sliced

Make the cabbage slaw by combining all the
ingredients in a large bowl. Whisk the dressing
ingredients together. Set aside.

Put all the ingredients for the marinade in a food
processor and pulse until smooth.

Heat a large non-stick frying pan with the olive oil
over medium–high heat. Add the chicken and season
it. Fry for 4 minutes, before adding 2 tablespoons of
the marinade and 1 tablespoon of water to the pan.
Reduce the heat slightly and turn the chicken over.
Leave for another 4 minutes, or until the chicken has
cooked through.

Remove the chicken from the heat and leave to rest.

Toss the cabbage slaw with the dressing and divide
between four serving bowls.

Top each bowl with the chicken, spring onion and
coriander leaves. Finish with the chilli, if using.

CABBAGE SLAW DRESSING (OPTIONAL)
✳ 1 tablespoon grated fresh ginger; 1 tablespoon
    sesame seeds; 60 ml (2 fl oz/¼ cup) rice vinegar;
    1½ tablespoons soy sauce; 60 ml (2 fl oz/¼ cup)
    sesame oil; 2 tablespoons coriander (cilantro)
    leaves, chopped; 1 tablespoon rice malt syrup;
    1 teaspoon peanut butter

You will have leftover marinade.
Store it in the fridge for
up to a week.

CHILLI LIME STEAK BOWL

DF // GF // NF // SF // P // 2703 KJ/646 CAL PER SERVE // SERVES 2

2 × 150 g (5¼ oz) beef eye fillet

MARINADE
1 teaspoon chilli powder
1 teaspoon ground cumin
1 teaspoon smoked paprika
½ teaspoon pink salt
good pinch of pepper
1 tablespoon lime zest (1 lime)
2 tablespoons lime juice
    (1 lime)
1 small garlic clove, crushed
1 teaspoon olive oil

BOWLS
1 teaspoon olive oil
1 medium red (Spanish) onion,
    finely sliced
½ green capsicum (pepper),
    cored and sliced
½ yellow capsicum (pepper),
    cored and sliced
100 g (3½ oz/⅔ cup) sweet
    red cherry tomatoes, halved
½ avocado, thinly sliced

RICE
1 x 250 g (8¾ oz) packet
    90-second long-grain
    microwave rice
1 teaspoon chopped coriander
    (cilantro) leaves
½ teaspoon butter
1 teaspoon lime zest
1 teaspoon lime juice
pink salt and cracked black
    pepper, to taste

Make the marinade by mixing all the ingredients in a bowl. Coat the steaks well, cover and refrigerate.

While the steaks are marinating, crack on with everything else. Heat the olive oil in a non-stick frying pan over medium heat and add the onion and capsicum. Fry until soft and the onion has slightly caramelised. Remove from the pan and set aside.

Add the steaks to the pan and cook for roughly 4 minutes on each side, or until cooked to your liking. Remove from the pan and leave to rest.

Next, microwave the rice according to the packet instructions. Combine the hot rice in a bowl with the coriander, butter, lime zest and juice. Season to taste.

Divide all the ingredients equally between two bowls and serve immediately.

TIP
✳ Although we have used eye fillet here, any cut will work, including scotch fillet, rump, etc.

15-MINUTE HUNGER-BUSTING PRAWN ZOODLES

DF // GF // SF // P // 2560 KJ/612 CAL PER SERVE // SERVES 2

500 g (1 lb 2 oz) raw prawns
   (shrimp), peeled and
   deveined
1½ tablespoons Cajun
   seasoning
2 garlic cloves, crushed
pink salt and freshly ground
   black pepper
2 tablespoons olive oil
200 g (7 oz/1⅓ cups) medley
   or sweet red cherry
   tomatoes, halved
4 medium zucchini
   (courgettes), spiralised into
   zoodles
90 g (3¼ oz/⅓ cup) ready-
   made basil pesto
2 tablespoons toasted pine
   nuts (optional)

In a large bowl, toss the prawns with the Cajun seasoning and garlic. Season with a good pinch of pink salt.

Heat one tablespoon of the olive oil in a non-stick frying pan over medium heat. Add the prawns, making sure they don't overlap in the pan. Cook for around 3 minutes on each side, or until just cooked through. Remove from the heat and transfer to a bowl.

Heat another tablespoon of olive oil in the same pan. Add the tomato and stir for a couple of minutes until softened. Add the zucchini zoodles and toss constantly for about 3 minutes until cooked through. Season with salt and pepper. Remove the mixture from the heat and add the pesto to the zoodles, stirring it through.

Put the zoodles into a serving bowl and top with the prawns. Scatter pine nuts over (if using). Serve immediately and enjoy!

You may not think that Cajun spice and pesto would work together but, surprisingly, they do!

TIP

* This is really easy to do as a one-dish wonder: just serve straight from the pan. Fewer dishes to wash up!

I'm obsessed with pesto pasta and prawn spaghetti—this is my fast and healthy combo!

– MAHA

HEAT OF THE NIGHT CHICKEN BOWL

DF // NF // 2109 KJ/504 CAL PER SERVE // SERVES 2

2 × 100 g (3½ oz) skinless
   chicken breasts
62 g (2¼ oz/½ cup) pearl (big)
   couscous
1 teaspoon olive oil
1 bunch broccolini
Greek-style yoghurt, to serve
   (optional)

MARINADE
2 teaspoons ground chilli
2 teaspoons Middle Eastern
   spice blend
2 teaspoons rice malt syrup
2 teaspoons lime zest
1 teaspoon ground sumac
½ teaspoon garlic salt
juice of ½ lime (reserve the lime
   halves after you've juiced)
1 tablespoon olive oil
pink salt and black pepper

ROAST VEGGIES
1 red (Spanish) onion,
   quartered
4 garlic cloves, unpeeled but
   smashed with the back of
   a knife
200 g (7 oz/1⅓ cups) punnet
   medley cherry tomatoes,
   halved
1 red capsicum (pepper),
   seeded and roughly
   chopped
1 teaspoon olive oil
pink salt and freshly ground
   black pepper

Preheat the oven to 200°C (400°F).

Mix all the ingredients for the marinade in a small bowl, then rub it all over the chicken, making sure it's well coated. Set aside.

Place the veggies in a roasting tray, drizzle with a teaspoon of olive oil, season with a little pink salt and pepper and mix well. Pop the reserved lime halves into the tray as well.

Place the chicken on top of the veggies and roast for 25–30 minutes, until the chicken has cooked through and the juices run clear.

While the chicken and veggies are in the oven, cook the pearl couscous according to the instructions on the packet.

Once the chicken is cooked, remove it from the roasting dish and leave to rest. Then return the veggies to the oven and turn up the heat to 230°C (450°F). Leave the veggies in the oven for another 8–10 minutes, or until they have nicely caramelised.

While the veggies are in the oven for the final 8–10 minutes, quickly blanch the broccolini in a bowl and cut the chicken into 1.5 cm (⅝ inch) slices. Divide the ingredients equally between two bowls. Add a dollop of yoghurt to the middle. *Enjoy!*

EGGS ELEVEN

DF // NF // SF // V // VG // 1862 KJ/445 CAL PER SERVE // SERVES 2

2 carrots, grated
4 radishes, grated or thinly
    sliced
½ avocado, thinly sliced
1 zucchini (courgette),
    spiralised
75 g (2¾ oz/1 cup) shredded
    red cabbage
½ cup cavolo nero, thinly sliced
¼ red (Spanish) onion, thinly
    sliced
2 tablespoons kimchi
2 eggs
1 x 250 g (8¾ oz) packet
    40-second microwave
    brown rice & quinoa
fresh red chilli, to serve
    (optional)

DRESSING (OPTIONAL)
2 tablespoons sesame seeds
2 tablespoons water
2½ tablespoons soy sauce
1 teaspoon rice malt syrup
½ tablespoon tahini
2 tablespoons rice vinegar
1 teaspoon chilli oil
pinch of salt

Make the dressing by combining all the ingredients in a bowl. Whisk and set aside.

Make the salad by dividing and placing the salad ingredients, together with the kimchi, around the sides of two serving bowls.

Poach or pan-fry the eggs (we like ours sunny-side up) and, during the last minute of cooking, microwave the rice & quinoa.

Place half the contents of the rice & quinoa packet into the middle of each prepared serving bowl. Top with one egg per bowl and garnish with the fresh sliced chilli (if using).

Drizzle dressing over the top of the eggs (note: we like to use HEAPS!) and serve immediately.

NOTES

* If you want to make this in mere minutes, use the grating attachment on your food processor to grate the cabbage, carrot, onion, radish and cavolo nero.

* *Leftover dressing* can be popped into a jar and stored in the fridge for up to a week.

* If you can't get your hands on cavolo nero, use kale ribbons.

If you're super-hungry,
add another egg
to each bowl.

DECONSTRUCTED RICE PAPER ROLL BOWL

DF // GF // NF // SF // 2385 KJ/570 CAL PER SERVE // SERVES 4

1 small barbecued chicken, skin
   removed and shredded
100 g/3½ oz vermicelli
   noodles, cooked (about
   2 cups)
2 Lebanese (short) cucumbers,
   sliced into matchsticks
100 g (3½ oz/1 cup) snow peas
   (mangetout), thinly sliced
1 large avocado, thinly sliced
2 carrots, grated
1 red capsicum (pepper),
   seeded and sliced into
   matchsticks
4 large leaves butter lettuce,
   sliced
1 mango, thinly sliced
25 g (1 oz/½ cup) basil leaves,
   sliced
10 g (¼ oz/½ cup mint leaves,
   sliced
1 red chilli, seeded and sliced
   (optional)
1 cup ready-made kimchi
handful of bean sprouts
   (optional)

DRESSING
80 ml (2½ fl oz/⅓ cup) sweet
   chilli sauce
2 tablespoons rice wine vinegar
1 tablespoon fish sauce
2 garlic cloves, crushed
1 tablespoon grated fresh
   ginger

Put all the dressing ingredients into a small bowl or
mixing jug and whisk to combine.

Arrange four serving bowls, dividing all ingredients
equally between them and placing each ingredient
around the side of the bowl.

Top with the chilli and sprouts (if using) and drizzle
with the dressing.

NOTES

✳ If you're extra-hungry, use more avocado.

✳ *A swap we like to make sometimes* is
   five cooked king prawns (shrimp) per serve from
   the local fishmonger, instead of chicken.

✳ If you don't want it spicy, drop the kimchi as well as
   the red chilli.

KALE AND MUSHROOM RICE BOWL

DF // NF // SF // 2017 KJ/482 CAL PER SERVE // SERVES 2

400 g (14 oz) tin of chickpeas,
    drained and rinsed
1 teaspoon olive oil
1 teaspoon smoked paprika
pink salt
2 teaspoons sesame oil
1 medium red (Spanish) onion,
    thinly sliced
2 garlic cloves, roughly
    chopped
100 g (3½ oz) shiitake
    mushrooms, sliced
150 g (5½ oz) oyster
    mushrooms, sliced
150 g (5½ oz) button or other
    white mushrooms, sliced
4 asparagus spears, chopped
1 spring onion, finely sliced
100 g (3½ oz/4 cups) kale
    ribbons (stalks removed,
    leaves sliced)
1 tablespoon lemon juice
2 tablespoons soy sauce
salt and freshly ground
    black pepper
1 teaspoon fish sauce
¼ teaspoon ground paprika
    (not smoked)
1 x 250 g (8¾ oz) packet
    90-second microwave rice
    & quinoa (or rice of your
    choice)

Preheat the oven to 200°C (400°F). Line a baking tray with baking paper.

In a small bowl, combine the chickpeas with the olive oil and smoked paprika. Season with a generous amount of pink salt and toss well.

Spread the chickpeas on the prepared baking tray and bake for about 18 minutes. Halfway through the cooking time, remove the tray from the oven, toss the chickpeas then return them to the oven. When cooked, set aside to cool.

While the chickpeas are in the oven, heat 1 teaspoon of sesame oil in a frying pan over medium heat. Add the onion to the pan and cook for about 4 minutes until softened.

Add the garlic, mushrooms, asparagus, spring onion and kale to the pan, together with the lemon juice and 1 tablespoon of the soy sauce. Season with salt and pepper.

Next make the optional dressing by combining 1 teaspoon sesame oil, 1 tablespoon soy sauce, the fish sauce and ground paprika in a jar. Seal with the lid and shake well.

Pop the rice & quinoa into the microwave and cook according to the packet instructions.

Divide the rice and mushroom and kale mixture between two serving bowls. Top with the chickpeas and drizzle with a little of the dressing. Enjoy!

FALAFEL BOWL WITH SPICY TAHINI DIP

GF // NF // SF // VG // 2515 KJ/601 CAL PER SERVE // SERVES 4

2 x 220 g (7 oz) ready-made
  falafel balls (from the fridge
  at the supermarket)

SPICY TAHINI DIP
130 g (4½ oz/½ cup) Greek-
  style yoghurt
2 tablespoons tahini
2 tablespoons flat-leaf (Italian)
  parsley, finely chopped
1 tablespoon lemon juice
1 tablespoon ready-made
  harissa paste

YOGHURT DRESSING
(OPTIONAL)
2 tablespoons olive oil
2 tablespoons Greek-style
  yoghurt
1 teaspoon za'atar

BOWL
2 Lebanese (short) cucumbers,
  quartered lengthways
1 cup diced tinned or vacuum-
  sealed beetroot (beets), cut
  into wedges
2 roasted red capsicum
  (peppers), sliced (from a jar)
200 g (7 oz) ready-made baba
  ghanoush
1 x 250 g (8¾ oz) packet
  40-second microwave
  brown rice & quinoa

Make the spicy tahini dip by mixing together all the ingredients in a bowl. Set aside.

Make the yoghurt dressing in a small bowl or mixing jug by combining all the ingredients.

Divide the cucumber, beetroot, red capsicum and baba ghanoush equally between two serving bowls.

Microwave the brown rice & quinoa according to the packet instructions.

Heat the falafel according to the packet instructions. Divide between the bowls, placing the falafel in the centre.

Drizzle the falafel with yoghurt dressing.

Serve immediately and enjoy with the spicy tahini dip.

Find the recipe for these delish choc caramel 'sambos' on page 239.

– CHAPTER FOUR –

snacks

EASY SUNDAY STARTER

GF // NF // SF // VG // 1933 KJ/462 CAL PER SERVE // **SERVES 6**

PLATTER

300 g (10½ oz) jar baby
    artichokes, drained
250 g (9 oz/2½ cups) pitted
    kalamata olives
1 bunch radishes, halved (leave
    tops on for colour)
400 g (14 oz) cherry tomato
    medley
2 large Lebanese (short)
    cucumbers, cut into sticks
8 whole baby carrots (leave
    tops on for colour)
8 small tinned or vacuum-
    sealed beetroot (beets),
    quartered
1 red capsicum (pepper), cut
    into chunks
1 yellow capsicum (pepper), cut
    into chunks
60 g (2¼ oz/½ cup)
    cauliflower florets
30 g (1 oz/½ cup) broccoli
    florets
1 tablespoon olive oil
180 g (6¼ oz) haloumi, cut into
    1 cm (⅜ inch) batons

Start by making the chilli lime dip. Put all the ingredients, except for the milk, in a food processor. Add a little of the milk and begin to blend. Keep slowly adding milk until you achieve a smooth consistency. From time to time you may need to stop the food processor and scrape the sides down. Taste and season with salt and pepper, if required. Once you have achieved the desired consistency for the dip, transfer it to a ramekin or small bowl.

Prepare the platter by arranging the vegetables and olives around the dip bowl, leaving enough space for the cooked haloumi.

Heat the olive oil in a non-stick frying pan over medium–high heat. Fry the haloumi for about a minute on each side until golden. Add it to the platter and serve!

CHILLI LIME DIP

✱ 190 g (6¾ oz/⅔ cup) Greek-style yoghurt;
2 ripe avocados, peeled and stones removed;
20 g (¾ oz/⅓ cup) coarsely chopped flat-leaf (Italian) parsley; 20 g (¾ oz/⅓ cup) coarsely chopped dill; 2 teaspoons dried chives; ½ red (Spanish) onion, coarsely chopped; 2 garlic cloves, crushed; zest and juice of 2 limes; 2 teaspoons chilli flakes; 185 ml (6 fl oz/¾ cup) milk; pink salt and freshly ground black pepper (to taste)

SAVOURY YOGHURT 4 WAYS

SERVES 1

1. BADA BING BADA BEANS

GF // NF // SF // VG
678 KJ/162 CAL PER SERVE

3 heaped tablespoons Greek-style yoghurt
167 g (6 oz/⅓ cup) tinned lima beans
    (butterbeans), drained and rinsed
45 g (1½ oz/⅓ cup) sweet red cherry
    tomatoes, diced
2 tablespoons chopped fresh flat-leaf
    (Italian) parsley
small pinch of cumin
1 teaspoon garlic-infused olive oil
pink salt and freshly ground black pepper
    (to taste)

Put the yoghurt into a bowl and top with
the beans, tomato and parsley. Sprinkle
the cumin over the top and drizzle with
the olive oil. Season with salt and pepper.
Serve immediately and enjoy!

2. HOT HARISSA

GF // NF // SF // VG
920 KJ/220 CAL PER SERVE

3 heaped tablespoons Greek-style yoghurt
1 teaspoon ready-made harissa paste
2 tablespoons Greek feta cheese, crumbled
small handful of mint leaves, finely sliced
1 teaspoon olive oil
pink salt and freshly ground black pepper
    (to taste)

Put the yoghurt into a bowl and top with
the harissa paste. Top with the feta and
mint. Drizzle with the olive oil and season
with salt and pepper. Serve immediately
and enjoy!

3. CAN'T BEET IT!

GF // NF // SF // VG
1222 KJ/292 CAL PER SERVE

3 heaped tablespoons Greek-style yoghurt
1 cooked beetroot (beet), chopped
   (vacuum-sealed pack), or ½ cup tinned
   diced beetroot
¼ avocado, sliced
2 walnuts, roughly chopped
1 teaspoon olive oil
pink salt and freshly ground black pepper
   (to taste)

Put the yoghurt into a bowl and top with
the beetroot and avocado. Scatter the
walnuts over the top, drizzle with olive oil
and season with salt and pepper. Serve
immediately and enjoy!

4. ZESTY ZA'ATAR

GF // NF // SF // VG
866 KJ/207 CAL PER SERVE

3 heaped tablespoons Greek-style yoghurt
70 g (2½ oz/½ cup) medley cherry
   tomatoes, halved
½ Lebanese (short) cucumber, chopped
¼ red (Spanish) onion, chopped
1 heaped teaspoon za'atar
¼ teaspoon sesame seeds
small handful of mint leaves, finely sliced
zest of ¼ lemon
1 teaspoon olive oil
pink salt and freshly ground black pepper
   (to taste)

Put the yoghurt into a bowl and top with
the cherry tomatoes, cucumber and
onion. Sprinkle the za'atar and sesame
seeds over the top, garnish with the mint
leaves and lemon zest. Finally, drizzle with
the olive oil and season with salt and
pepper. Serve immediately and enjoy!

1. bada bing bada beans

2. hot harissa

3. can't beet it!

4. zesty za'atar

LEMON PROTEIN BALLS

DF // GF // V // VG // P // 694 KJ/166 CAL PER BALL // **MAKES 12**

155 g (5½ oz/1 cup) raw
   cashews
90 g (3¼ oz/1 cup) desiccated
   (shredded) coconut, plus
   extra for coating
zest and juice of 2 lemons
¼ teaspoon vanilla bean paste
2 tablespoons vanilla protein
   powder
2 tablespoons rice malt syrup

Line a baking tray with baking paper. Put all the ingredients into a food processor and blend until you get a sticky mixture.

Shape the mix into balls. Roll the balls in the extra desiccated coconut and set them out on the prepared tray. Transfer to the fridge to set, about 1 hour.

To get the real lemon flavour, these are best consumed at room temperature. They will keep for a few days, stored in an airtight container in the fridge.

SWEET POTATO TOAST 8 WAYS

SERVES 1 (1 SLICE = 1 SERVE)

TOAST
sweet potato, sliced into 5 mm
(¼ inch) thick slices

Put the sweet potato slices into the toaster the way you would regular bread. How long you leave them in the toaster will depend on the type of appliance you have. For us, it is two rounds in the toaster on the number 5 setting. Just make sure you keep an eye on yours, particularly the first time you do it, to see what works best.

Serve hot with one of our delicious topping suggestions (see opposite).

Trust us on this one . . . it's so super-skinny on the kilojoules (calories), deliciously healthy and satisfying that you'll be swapping your regular toast for sweet potato 'toast' all the time.

1. CHOCOYEAHBABY

DF // GF // SF // V // VG
703 KJ/168 CAL PER SERVE

Spread the 'toast' with 1 tablespoon natural choc-hazelnut spread (found in the health-food aisle at the supermarket) and top with 1 teaspoon desiccated (shredded) coconut.

2. FRIED EGGS 'N' SPICE

DF // GF // NF // SF // VG // P
506 KJ/121 CAL PER SERVE

Perfect for a weekend morning. Pan-fry an egg and place it on top of your slice of 'toast'. Drizzle with 1 teaspoon sriracha, or to taste.

3. ZA'ATAR

DF // GF // NF // SF // V // VG // P
954 KJ/228 CAL PER SERVE

Smash half an avocado in a small bowl with a squeeze of lemon juice. Add about 1 teaspoon of za'atar. If you want a little hit of chilli (which we love), add a sprinkle of dried chilli flakes to the mix.

4. OLIVE YOU

DF // GF // NF // SF // V // VG
523 KJ/125 CAL PER SERVE

Cover the 'toast' with 1 tablespoon of hummus (more or less to taste). Finely chop 4 kalamata olives and 1 tablespoon of parsley leaves and spread on top of the hummus.

5. SMASHED PEAS

GF // NF // SF // VG
899 KJ/215 CAL PER SERVE

Place 110 g (3¾ oz/¾ cup) of frozen peas in a small bowl and add a little water in the bottom. Microwave until cooked through. Drain, then smash the peas in the bowl with the back of a fork. Add 2 heaped tablespoons of goat's feta cheese. Season with salt and pepper.

6. SMOKED SALMON

DF // GF // NF // SF // V // VG // P
740 KJ/177 CAL PER SERVE

Spread the 'toast' with 1 tablespoon cream cheese and top with 30 g (1 oz) smoked salmon. We love to add some thin slices of red (Spanish) onion and freshly cracked black pepper. Yum!

7. PBM

DF // GF // V // VG
791 KJ/189 CAL PER SERVE

Spread with natural almond or peanut butter, top with banana slices and a drizzle of maple syrup.

8. SAY CHEESE

GF // NF // SF // VG
661 KJ/158 CAL PER SERVE

Slice 2 small balls (40 g/1½ oz) of baby bocconcini and place on top of the sweet potato 'toast'. Pop under a grill for 2 minutes or until the cheese melts. Top with a few sliced cherry tomatoes.

1. chocoyeahbaby

2. fried eggs 'n' spice

3. za'atar

4. olive you

5. smashed peas

6. smoked salmon

7. PBM

8. say cheese

BROCCAMOLE

DF // GF // NF // SF // V // VG // P // 368 KJ/88 CAL PER SERVE // **SERVES 6**

90 g (3¼ oz/1½ cups) coarsely
  chopped broccoli
125 g (4½ oz/1 cup) coarsely
  chopped cauliflower
2 small avocados, peeled and
  stones removed
1 garlic clove, crushed
2 tablespoons coarsely
  chopped coriander (cilantro)
  leaves
2 spring onions (scallions),
  coarsely chopped
1 fresh long red chilli, sliced and
  seeds removed
juice of 1 lime (2 tablespoons)
½ teaspoon pink salt
pepper, to taste

Steam the broccoli and cauliflower in the microwave with half a cup of water (125 ml/4 fl oz) for 3 minutes, or until the vegetables are easily cut with a knife. Set aside to cool for a few minutes.

Put all the ingredients into a food processor, season with pink salt and freshly ground black pepper and blend until the dip reaches the desired consistency (we like ours a little chunky).

Serve with crudités or crispbread.

Yes, it's broccoli guacamole—but trust us on this one, it's good! Plus it's an easy and delicious way to sneak in those all-important veggies for kids. Just drop the chilli from the recipe.

— MAHA

You guac me up!

1.   2.   3.

4.   5.

6.   7.   8.

AMP'ED UP AVOCADO

½ medium avocado per person

1. POMEGRANATE POP

GF // NF // SF // VG

1033 KJ/247 CAL PER SERVE

2 tbsp labneh topped with 1 tsp
pomegranate seeds and 1 tsp chopped
pistachios, drizzled with 1 tsp honey

2. ALWAYS BE GRAPEFUL

GF // NF // SF // VG

908 KJ/217 CAL PER SERVE

¼ grapefruit, sliced, with 1 tbsp Greek-
style yoghurt, sprinkled with fresh pepper
and ½ tsp chia seeds

3. ADD THE BEET

GF // NF // SF // VG

1196 KJ/286 CAL PER SERVE

75 g (2¾ oz/¼ cup) cottage cheese with
2 beetroot (beet) slices, sprinkled with
1 tsp pumpkin seeds (pepitas)

4. SOUNDS FISHY

DF // GF // NF // SF // P

933 KJ/223 CAL PER SERVE

40 g (1½ oz/¼ cup) chopped sashimi-
grade tuna sprinkled with ½ tsp black
and white sesame seeds and 1 tsp
pickled ginger

5. NO BETTER THAN FETA

GF // NF // SF // VG

1129 KJ/270 CAL PER SERVE

35 g (1¼ oz/¼ cup) crumbled feta
cheese; 4 cherry tomatoes, quartered;
and 2 tsp shredded mint leaves

6. YOU'RE RADISHING

GF // NF // SF // VG

1050 KJ/251 CAL PER SERVE

1 small radish, sliced; 2 tbsp goat's
cheese; ¼ cup steamed peas; ½ tsp
lime juice; and 1 tsp shredded mint

7. EASY CAPRESE

GF // NF // SF // VG

954 KJ/228 CAL PER SERVE

caramelised balsamic vinegar; 20 g
(¾ oz) bocconcini; ½ roma (plum)
tomato, sliced; 2 tsp basil leaves

8. SPICE UP MY LIFE

DF // GF // NF // SF // V // VG // P

418 KJ/100 CAL PER SERVE

⅛ red (Spanish) onion, finely chopped;
juice of ½ lime; 2 tbsp chopped coriander
(cilantro) leaves; 1 fresh jalapeño chilli,
finely sliced

TWO-MINUTE STRAWBERRY GELATO

DF // GF // NF // SF // V // VG // P // 201 KJ/48 CAL PER SERVE // **SERVES 4**

600 g (1 lb 5 oz/4 cups) frozen
   strawberries
80 ml (2½ fl oz/⅓ cup) orange
   juice
mint leaves, to serve (optional)
seeds of 1 pomegranate, to
   serve (optional)

Blend the strawberries and orange juice in a food processor until well combined (you can use a blender if yours can blend frozen ingredients).

Top with the mint leaves or pomegranate seeds (if using). Serve immediately and enjoy!

This is a hands-down favourite with both the kids and the grown-ups! I've found I have to be quick if I want any before my mini me, Annabelle, devours it!

— SALLY

SOCCA FLATBREADS 4 WAYS

MAKES ABOUT 8-12 FLATBREADS

270 g (9½ oz/2¼ cups)
    chickpea flour (besan)
1½ tablespoons olive oil
¼ teaspoon salt, or less if
    you prefer
olive oil spray, or coconut
    oil spray

Whisk together the chickpea flour, 500 ml (17 fl oz/ 2 cups) of water, the olive oil and salt in a large bowl, ensuring that there are no lumps.

Spray a small non-stick frying pan or cast-iron skillet with the olive oil or coconut oil spray and heat over medium–high heat.

Add about 2 tablespoons of the batter to the pan and leave to cook for 2–3 minutes, then flip over carefully. Cook for another 1–2 minutes, until the flatbreads have a nice golden colour (the way pancakes look). Remove from the heat and serve immediately with your favourite topping.

Socca are gluten-free flatbreads made from chickpea flour (besan), and they taste delicious with a whole variety of toppings. Those suggested here are a few of our favourites, but feel free to get creative! Chickpeas are full of protein, fibre and iron and are low in fat. What a fabulous superfood!

– MAHA

1. LABNEH LOVE

GF // NF // SF // VG
665 KJ/159 CAL PER SERVE

large handful rocket (arugula) leaves
1 tablespoon olive oil
1 small jar labneh (around 300 g/10½ oz)
12 kalamata olives, pitted and halved

In a small bowl, toss the rocket with the olive oil. Spread the labneh generously over the flatbreads. Top with the rocket and olives.

2. BANGIN' BEET

GF // NF // SF // VG
824 KJ/197 CAL PER SERVE

3 whole tinned or vacuum-sealed beetroot (beets)
250 g (9 oz) cream cheese
salt and freshly ground black pepper

Slice the beetroot into thin slices, about 5 mm (¼ inch) thick. Spread the cream cheese over the flatbread and top with the beetroot slices. Season with salt and pepper.

3. PBH

DF // GF // VG
1381 KJ/330 CAL PER SERVE

2 bananas
1 small jar (around 325 g/10½ oz) natural peanut butter (from the health-food aisle)
3 tablespoons honey or maple syrup

Slice the banana into thin slices, about 5 mm (¼ inch) thick. Spread the peanut butter onto the socca, top with banana slices and drizzle the honey (or maple syrup) over the top. Top with blueberries (optional).

4. AVOCADO SALSA

DF // GF // NF // SF // V // VG // P
648 KJ/155 CAL PER SERVE

1 avocado, peeled and stone removed
1 tomato, chopped
½ red (Spanish) onion, chopped
2 tablespoons lemon juice
1 teaspoon chilli flakes
salt and freshly ground black pepper

In a small bowl, mash the avocado. Add the tomato and onion and mix well. Add a squeeze of lemon juice, scatter with chilli flakes and season with salt and pepper.

1. labneh love

2. bangin' beet

3. PBH

4. avocado salsa

WHIP IT AND DIP IT

GF // NF // SF // VG // 1983 KJ/474 CAL PER SERVE // **SERVES 2**
991 KJ/237 CAL PER SERVE // **SERVES 4**

240 g (8¾ oz) goat's feta
cheese
1½ tablespoons olive oil
80 g (2¾ oz) baby spinach
leaves
2 garlic cloves
1 tablespoon chopped basil
leaves
zest of 1 small lemon
salt and freshly ground black
pepper (optional)

Place all the ingredients in a food processor and blend until well combined. You want to achieve a nice whipped consistency. Season with salt and pepper if desired (we generally don't as the feta is quite salty already).

NOTE

✶ You'll have to scrape down the sides of the food processor a few times as you go, to ensure that the mixture is well combined.

EGGCEPTIONAL EGGS 12 WAYS

1 boiled egg per person

1. DUKKAH
DF // GF // SF // VG // P
314 KJ/75 CAL PER SERVE

1 tsp za'atar or dukkah

2. HARISSA
DF // GF // NF // SF // V // VG // P
326 KJ/78 CAL PER SERVE

1 tsp ready-made harissa paste

3. SPANISH CORN
DF // GF // NF // SF // V // VG // P
339 KJ/81 CAL PER SERVE

1 tbsp corn kernels, 1 chopped cherry tomato, 1 tsp diced red onion, 1 tsp coriander (cilantro), squeeze lime juice, salt and pepper

4. PROSCIUTTO
DF // GF // NF // SF // P
489 KJ/117 CAL PER SERVE

1 slice prosciutto, 5 g (⅛ oz) rocket

5. KIMCHI
DF // GF // NF // SF // VG // P
284 KJ/68 CAL PER SERVE

1 tbsp kimchi

6. PESTO
GF // SF // VG
397 KJ/95 CAL PER SERVE

1 tsp pesto

7. SMOKED TROUT
DF // GF // NF // SF // P
456 KJ/109 CAL PER SERVE

1 slice smoked trout, 1 tsp fresh dill

8. FETA + OLIVE
GF // NF // SF
401 KJ/96 CAL PER SERVE

Persian feta cheese, 2 tsp black olive slices

9. RADISH
DF // GF // NF // SF // V // VG // P
276 KJ/66 CAL PER SERVE

truffle salt, 1 slice of radish

10. STICKY ONION
DF // GF // NF // SF // V // VG // P
464 KJ/111 CAL PER SERVE

1 tbsp caramelised onion (see p. 236), ½ tsp chopped chives

11. SMOKY AVO
DF // GF // NF // SF // V // VG // P
498 KJ/119 CAL PER SERVE

¼ avocado, mashed with smoked paprika

12. RED PEPPER
DF // GF // NF // SF // V // VG // P
305 KJ/73 CAL PER SERVE

1 tbsp chopped marinated red capsicum

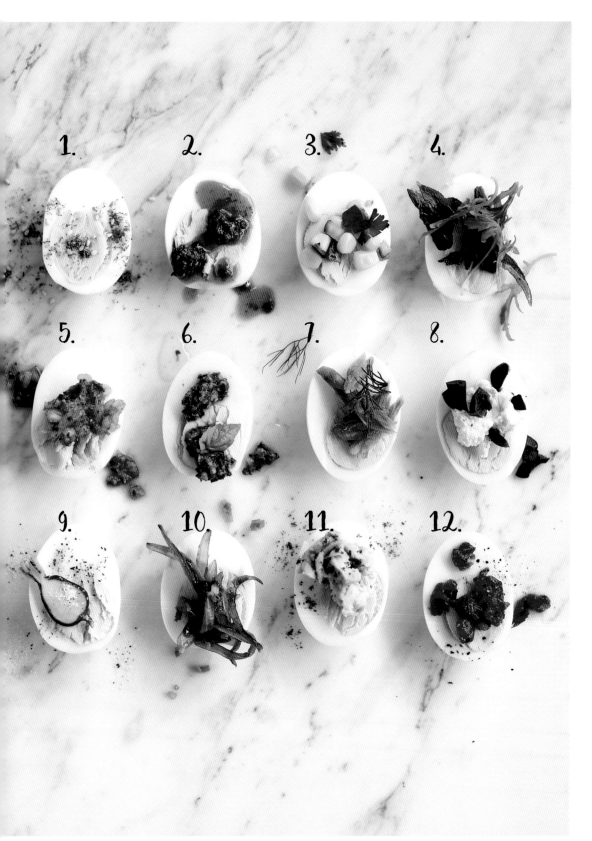

RAW BOUNTYFUL SLICE

DF // GF // NF // V // VG // 1276 KJ/305 CAL PER SERVE
MAKES ABOUT 16 SQUARES

260 g (9¼ oz/4 cups)
   desiccated (shredded)
   coconut
125 ml (4 fl oz/½ cup)
   unsweetened tinned
   coconut milk
125 ml (4 fl oz/½ cup) rice malt
   syrup
80 ml (2½ fl oz/⅓ cup)
   coconut oil

TOPPING
160 ml (5¼ fl oz) coconut oil
160 ml (5¼ fl oz) rice malt
   syrup
40 g (1½ oz/⅓ cup) cacao
   powder

Line a 16 cm (6 inch) square shallow cake tin with baking paper.

Start by making the base. Put all the base ingredients in a food processor and mix until thoroughly combined. You might need to stop and scrape the sides down a few times during this process.

Put the base mix into the tin. Use the back of a spoon (or your hands) to ensure that the base is evenly distributed across the bottom of the cake tin. Freeze to set.

Next, make the topping by putting all the ingredients into the food processor and pulsing until combined. Spread the topping over the frozen base and return the tin to the freezer for about 1 hour.

Remove from the freezer and cut into 4 cm (1½ inch) squares.

NOTE
✳ These actually improve with time. They'll last for a couple of weeks in the fridge and the coconut flavour becomes enhanced as time goes on.

CHIA KIWI POPS

DF // GF // NF // V // VG // P // 586 KJ/140 CAL PER SERVE // **MAKES 5**

270 ml (9½ fl oz) unsweetened
   tinned coconut milk
40 g (1½ oz/¼ cup) chia seeds
2 tablespoons agave nectar
1 kiwifruit, peeled and thinly
   sliced

In a large bowl or mixing jug combine the coconut milk, chia seeds and agave nectar. Taste and add more sweetener if desired.

Press the kiwifruit slices into popsicle moulds and pour in the coconut milk mixture. Freeze until set, about 4 hours.

CHOCOLICIOUS FUDGE BALLS

DF // GF // NF // SF // V // VG // P // 297 KJ/71 CAL PER SERVE // **MAKES ABOUT 20**

480 g (1 lb 1oz/3 cups) pitted
  medjool dates
1½ tablespoons cacao powder
  (you can also use
  unsweetened cocoa
  powder)
pinch of pink salt
moist coconut flakes, to serve
  (optional)

Blend the dates, cacao and salt in a food processor until smooth. Freeze the mixture for a few hours before rolling into balls.

Roll the balls in the coconut flakes (if using). Transfer to the fridge to set, about 1 hour.

Store in an airtight container in the fridge or freezer for up to 1 week.

TOAST OF THE TOWN

SERVES 2

1. DO THE MASH

DF // NF // SF // V // VG
1297 KJ/310 CAL PER SERVE

2 slices sourdough toast, 2 tbsp coconut oil mashed with 1 banana, 2 strawberries (sliced), 1 tsp coconut flakes

2. BEET IT, CHICK

DF // GF // NF // SF // V // VG // P
1025 KJ/245 CAL PER SERVE

2 slices sourdough toast, ½ cup beetroot hummus, ¼ cup tinned chickpeas (rinsed and drained), 1 tbsp chopped mint

3. FOR THE LOVE OF LABNEH

VG // 1129 KJ/270 CAL PER SERVE

2 slices sourdough toast, ½ cup labneh, 2 tbsp slivered almonds, 2 tbsp pomegranate seeds, 2 tsp honey

4. BERRY YUM

NF // SF // VG
1540 KJ/368 CAL PER SERVE

2 slices sourdough toast, 120 g (4¼ oz/ ½ cup) cream cheese, 155 g (5½ oz/ 1 cup) blueberries, 1 tbsp chia seeds

5. FIRE STARTER

DF // NF // SF // V // VG
1293 KJ/309 CAL PER SERVE

2 slices sourdough toast, 2 tbsp ready-made harissa paste, 1 mashed avocado, 1 tbsp chopped mint

6. GREEN EGGS

DF // NF // SF // VG
711 KJ/170 CAL PER SERVE

2 slices sourdough toast; 90 g (3¼ oz/ 2 cups) baby spinach leaves, sautéed with 1 tsp crushed garlic; soft-fried egg

7. HOLY GUACAMOLE

NF // SF // VG
1058 KJ/253 CAL PER SERVE

2 slices sourdough toast, ½ mashed avocado, 115 g (4 oz/½ cup) ricotta cheese, 1 finely chopped red bird's eye chilli, ½ tbsp finely grated lemon zest, salt and pepper

8. CHOC BANANA

DF // V // VG
1209 KJ/289 CAL PER SERVE

2 slices sourdough toast, 2 tbsp cocoa almond butter, 1 sliced banana, 1 tsp cacao nibs, 2 tsp maple/rice malt syrup

9. FIGALICIOUS

SF // V
2749 KJ/350 CAL PER SERVE

2 slices sourdough toast, 120 g (4¼ oz/ ½ cup) cream cheese, 2 sliced figs, 1 tbsp chopped pistachios

1.

2.

3.

4.

5.

6.

7.

8.

9.

SALTED CARAMEL DELIGHTS

GF // SF // VG // 535 KJ/128 CAL PER SERVE // **MAKES 25**

320 g (11¼ oz/2 cups) pitted
  medjool dates
310 g (11 oz/2 cups)
  macadamia nuts
2 teaspoons vanilla bean paste
½ teaspoon salt
1 tablespoon milk (we use cow's
  milk but almond milk also
  works)
pinch of sea salt

In a food processor, blend the dates, macadamia nuts, vanilla bean paste and salt. When it's well combined, add the milk and continue to process until the mixture is sticky.

Spoon into a 16 cm (6 inch) cake tin, lined with baking paper (or use a tin with a removable base), press down and then sprinkle with sea salt and freeze for 3–4 hours until firm.

TIP

✳ These are best kept in the freezer for up to 2 weeks.

SUPERFOOD ENERGY BALLS

DF // GF // V // VG // 636 KJ/152 CAL PER SERVE // **MAKES ABOUT 15**

100 g (3½ oz/1 cup) almond
    meal
135 g (4¾ oz/1½ cups)
    desiccated (shredded)
    coconut, plus extra for
    coating, if desired
3 teaspoons SWIISH DELIISH
    Super Green Superfood
    Powder (see page 103), plus
    extra for coating, if desired
zest and juice of 1 lime
60 ml (2 fl oz/¼ cup) coconut
    oil
80 ml (2½ fl oz/⅓ cup) rice
    malt syrup

Combine all the ingredients in a bowl and mix together well. Shape into balls, and roll in extra coconut plus extra superfood powder. Transfer to the fridge for about an hour to set.

Store in an airtight container in the fridge for up to 1 week.

TIP

✳ SWIISH DELIISH Super Green Superfood Powder is available from shop.swiish.com.

HUMMUS 8 WAYS

SERVES 2

BASE
100 g (3½ oz) ready-made
    hummus
pink salt and freshly ground
    black pepper (to taste)

Spread hummus on a plate and top with one of our delicious suggestions below.

1. HARISSA

GF // NF // SF // VG
684 KJ/163 CAL PER SERVE

1 tablespoon ready-made harissa paste
1 teaspoon finely chopped red (Spanish)
    onion
1 teaspoon finely chopped mint leaves
1 teaspoon Greek-style yoghurt

2. PINE NUTS + PARSLEY

DF // GF // SF // V // VG
692 KJ/165 CAL PER SERVE

2 tablespoons chopped, flat-leaf (Italian)
    parsley leaves
2 teaspoons toasted pine nuts
2 tablespoons fresh lemon juice
pomegranate seeds (optional)

3. ROASTED RED PEPPER

DF // GF // NF // SF // V // VG
830 KJ/198 CAL PER SERVE

2 tablespoons finely chopped ready-made
    roasted red capsicum (pepper)
6 pitted kalamata olives (or olives of your
    choice)
1 teaspoon olive oil
1 tablespoon finely chopped mint leaves

2.

1.

3.

4.

4. ZA'ATAR

DF // GF // SF // V // VG
705 KJ/168 CAL PER SERVE

1 teaspoon za'atar
2 teaspoons finely chopped preserved lemon
1 teaspoon olive oil
1 teaspoon chopped cashews
chilli flakes, to taste

5. RAD-O-CADO

DF // GF // NF // SF // V // VG
922 KJ/220 CAL PER SERVE

2 small radishes, finely chopped
½ avocado, mashed
1 tablespoon finely sliced mint leaves
squeeze of fresh lemon juice

6. PESTO

GF // SF // VG
711 KJ/170 CAL PER SERVE

½ teaspoon ready-made pesto
4 cherry tomatoes, quartered
4 slices bocconcini

7. POMEGRANATE

DF // GF // NF // SF // V // VG
581 KJ/139 CAL PER SERVE

½ teaspoon pomegranate molasses
2 teaspoons finely chopped preserved
    lemons
pomegranate seeds, for garnish
    (optional)

8. FRESH GREEK

DF // GF // NF // SF // V // VG
663 KJ/158 CAL PER SERVE

½ roma (plum) tomato, chopped
½ Lebanese (short) cucumber, chopped
1 tablespoon finely chopped red (Spanish)
    onion
1 tablespoon finely chopped mint leaves
½ teaspoon olive oil, drizzled on top

7.

6.

5.

8.

raspberry coconut balls

craving-buster tahini balls

CRAVING-BUSTER TAHINI BALLS

DF // GF // VG // 661 KJ/158 CAL PER SERVE // **MAKES ABOUT 16**

90 g (3¼ oz/1 cup) desiccated
(shredded) coconut, plus
extra for coating
155 g (5½ oz/1 cup) dried
apricots, roughly chopped
135 g (4¾ oz/½ cup) tahini
90 g (3¼ oz/¼ cup) honey
40 g (1½ oz/¼ cup) almonds,
coarsely chopped

Mix all the ingredients together in a bowl. Taste and add a little extra honey if you like it sweeter. Shape the mixture into balls, then roll in the extra desiccated coconut. Transfer to the fridge to set, about 1 hour.

These balls can be stored in an airtight container in the fridge for up to 1 week.

RASPBERRY COCONUT BALLS

DF // NF // SF // V // VG // P // 368 KJ/88 CAL PER SERVE // **MAKES 12**

185 g (6½ oz/1½ cups) frozen
raspberries, defrosted
105 g (3½ oz/1 cup) rolled
(porridge) oats
45 g (1½ oz/½ cup) desiccated
(shredded) coconut
2 tablespoons maple syrup
1 tablespoon coconut oil

Line a baking tray with baking paper. Slightly smash the raspberries in a large bowl. Add all the remaining ingredients and mix well.

Roll into balls and set the balls out on the prepared tray. Transfer to the fridge to set, about 1 hour.

These will keep for a few days, stored in an airtight container in the refrigerator.

GET FIGGY WITH IT FLATBREAD

NF // SF // 1678 KJ/401 CAL PER SERVE // **SERVES 4**

¾ cup ready-made
    caramelised onion
4 pitta bread rounds
65 g (2½ oz/½ cup) crumbled
    Danish or Greek feta cheese
4 figs, sliced
large handful of rocket
    (arugula) leaves
1 tablespoon olive oil
1 teaspoon balsamic vinegar
    (optional)
pink salt and freshly ground
    black pepper (to taste)
4 slices proscuitto

If you want to make your own caramelised onion, here's how.

Preheat the oven to 200°C (400°F). Line a baking tray with baking paper.

Spread the caramelised onion over the pitta bread. Top with half the crumbled feta and the fig slices and place on the prepared baking tray.

Bake for about 10 minutes, or until the pitta bread is crisp at the edges.

While the flatbread is cooking, toss the rocket in a bowl with the olive oil and the balsamic vinegar (if using). Season with salt and pepper.

Remove the flatbread from the oven and top with a slice of proscuitto and the rocket. Add the remaining feta.

Serve immediately.

CARAMELISED ONION

2 tablespoons olive oil
3 brown onions, finely sliced
1 teaspoon pink salt
2 tablespoons brown sugar
cracked black pepper, to taste
1 tablespoon balsamic vinegar

Heat the olive oil in a non-stick frying pan over low heat. Add the onion and sprinkle with the pink salt. Cook for about 10–12 minutes, stirring occasionally, until the onions become very soft and a translucent gold in colour.

Add the sugar, pepper and balsamic vinegar and continue to cook for about another 10–15 minutes, stirring until the onion becomes quite sticky and dark. Store in an airtight jar in the fridge for up to 1 week.

CHOC CARAMEL 'SAMBOS'

DF // GF // SF // V // VG // P // 1012 KJ/242 CAL PER SERVE // **MAKES ABOUT 12**

15 medjool dates, pitted
110 g (3¾ oz/1 cup) hazelnut
    meal
4 tablespoons cacao powder
    (you can also use
    unsweetened cocoa
    powder)
small pinch of pink salt

FILLING
80 g (2¾ oz/½ cup) cashews
    (or nuts of your choice)
8 medjool dates, pitted
2 teaspoons coconut oil

Line a baking tray with baking paper. In a food processor, blend 12 of the dates, the hazelnut meal, cacao powder and salt until a thick mixture forms. Add 3 more dates to the food processor and blend again until the mixture is sticky and holds together well.

Using your hands, make 24 small rounds of 'bikkies'. You want these to be evenly sized. Place them on the prepared tray.

To make the filling, put the cashews into the food processor and blend to a fine texture. Add the dates and coconut oil and blend until well combined and the mixture becomes sticky.

Spread the filling onto half of the bikkies, then top with the other half of the bikkies—these are your sambos!

Pop them into the fridge or freezer for at least 30 minutes to cool and set before serving.

TIPS

✳ To get the sambos perfectly round quickly, the easiest way is to turn each one onto its side and roll it like a little wheel, forwards and backwards.

✳ These will keep in an airtight container in the freezer for 2 weeks.

FROZEN YOGHURT BERRIES 3 WAYS

SERVES 2

1. QUICK AND EASY

DF // NF // VG
456 KJ/109 CAL PER SERVE

130 g (4½ oz/½ cup) Greek-style yoghurt
2 teaspoons rice malt syrup
60 g (2¼ oz) blueberries (about half a
    punnet)

Line a baking tray with baking paper. Mix
together the yoghurt and rice malt syrup
in a bowl.

Dip the blueberries in the yoghurt mix
and ensure they're well coated. Place
on the prepared tray, ensuring that none
are touching or overlapping. Freeze for
1½ hours or until frozen.

2. CHIA SQUAD

GF // NF // VG
485 KJ/116 CAL PER SERVE

130 g (4½ oz/½ cup) Greek-style yoghurt
2 teaspoons rice malt syrup
60 g (2¼ oz) blueberries (about half a
    punnet)
1 teaspoon black and white chia seeds

Line a baking tray with baking paper. Mix
the yoghurt and rice malt syrup in a bowl.

Dip the blueberries in the yoghurt mix
and ensure they're well coated. Place on
the prepared tray, ensuring that none are
touching or overlapping.

Sprinkle with the chia seeds, ensuring that
all the blueberries are covered.

Freeze for 1½ hours or until frozen.

3. STRAWBERRY FIELDS

GF // NF // VG
498 KJ/118 CAL PER SERVE

130 g (4½ oz/½ cup) Greek-style yoghurt
2 teaspoons rice malt syrup
½ vanilla bean, seeds scraped
200 g (7 oz/1⅓ cups) strawberries (about
    1 punnet), hulled

Line a baking tray with baking paper. Mix
together the yoghurt, rice malt syrup and
vanilla seeds in a bowl.

Dip the strawberries in the yoghurt mix
and ensure they're well coated. Lay on
the prepared tray, ensuring that none
are touching or overlapping.

Freeze for 1½ hours or until frozen.

These come with a big warning: they're very more-ish! Don't say we didn't warn you!

3. strawberry fields

1. quick and easy

2. chia squad

I like to put some cacao nibs or puffed quinoa on the top of the popsicles once you've poured the mix in— it makes the popsicles look that little bit prettier.

– MAHA

SUPER GREEN SUPERFOOD POPS

DF // GF // NF // SF // V // VG // P // 226 KJ/54 CAL PER SERVE // **MAKES ABOUT 12**

315 g (11¼ oz/1 cup) frozen
  mango pieces
1 banana
1 avocado
45 g (1½ oz/1 cup) baby
  spinach leaves
25 g (1 oz/1 cup) kale ribbons
  (stalks removed, leaves
  sliced)
500 ml (17 fl oz/2 cups) water
2 teaspoons SWIISH DELIISH
  Super Green Superfood
  Powder (see page 103)
1 tablespoon stevia, or more
  to taste

Blend all the ingredients.

Taste and add extra sweetener if desired.

Pour into popsicle moulds and freeze until set,
 about 4 hours.

NUTRITIONAL CHART

RECIPE	DF	GF	NF	SF	V	VG	P	Kj	Cal	Page
ACAI WHAT YOU DID THERE BOWL	√	√	√	√	√	√	√	945	226	91
ADD THE BEET AVOCADO		√	√	√		√		1196	286	207
ALL-VEGGIE ALL-ROUNDER, THE	√	√	√	√	√	√	√	644	154	62
ALL WHITE ALL RIGHT		√	√	√		√		640	153	84
ALWAYS BE GRAPEFUL AVOCADO		√	√	√		√		908	217	207
ANNIHILATOR, THE	√	√	√	√	√	√	√	284	68	116
ANTI-INFLAMMATORY TURMERIC TONIC	√	√	√		√	√	√	211	50	117
ASIAN KAZOODLE SALAD	√	√	√	√	√	√	√	1117	267	127
AVOCADO SALSA SOCCA FLATBREAD	√	√	√	√	√	√	√	648	155	211
'AVO GREAT DAY GREEN BOWL	√	√		√	√	√	√	1217	291	88
BADA BING BADA BEANS SAVOURY YOGHURT		√	√	√		√		678	162	194
BANGIN' BEET SOCCA FLATBREAD		√	√	√		√		824	197	211
BEET IT, CHICK TOAST	√	√	√	√	√	√	√	1025	245	226
BEET IT SALAD		√	√	√		√		1699	406	145
BERRY DELICIOUS BOWL		√		√		√		1006	240	65
BERRY YUM TOAST			√	√		√		1540	368	226
BROCCAMOLE	√	√	√	√	√	√	√	368	88	204
CAN'T BEET IT! SAVOURY YOGHURT		√	√	√		√		1222	292	195
CHIA KIWI POPS	√	√	√		√	√	√	586	140	222
CHIA SQUAD	√	√		√	√	√	√	1163	278	69
CHIA SQUAD FROZEN YOGHURT BERRIES	√		√			√		485	116	240
CHILLI LIME STEAK BOWL	√	√	√	√			√	2703	646	177
CHOC BANANA TOAST	√				√	√		1209	289	226
CHOC CARAMEL 'SAMBOS'	√	√		√	√	√	√	1012	242	239
CHOC FULL OF VEGGIES WHIPPED BOWL	√	√	√	√	√	√	√	1084	259	78
CHOCOLICIOUS FUDGE BALLS	√	√	√	√	√	√	√	297	71	225
CHOCOYEAHBABY SWEET POTATO TOAST	√	√		√	√	√		703	168	201
COCONUT CHIA BOWL	√	√	√	√	√	√	√	1232	294	159
CRAVING-BUSTER TAHINI BALLS	√	√				√		661	158	235
DEBRIEF SALAD, THE			√	√		√		2102	502	132
DECONSTRUCTED RICE PAPER ROLL BOWL	√	√	√	√				2385	570	185
DETOX-DEBLOAT-ENERGISER	√	√	√	√	√	√	√	648	155	92

RECIPE	DF	GF	NF	SF	V	VG	P	Kj	Cal	Page
DIGESTION BOOSTER SHOT	√	√	√	√	√	√	√	84	20	116
DO THE MASH TOAST	√		√	√	√	√		1297	310	226
DUKKAH EGGS	√	√		√		√	√	314	75	218
EASY CAPRESE AVOCADO		√	√	√		√		954	228	207
EASY SUNDAY STARTER		√	√	√		√		1933	462	192
EAT THE RAINBOW SALAD	√	√		√	√	√	√	933	223	120
EGGS ELEVEN	√		√	√	√	√		1862	445	182
E-V-A (ENERGY VITALITY ALKALINE) SUPERFOOD SHOT	√	√	√	√	√	√	√	54	13	117
FALAFEL BOWL WITH SPICY TAHINI DIP		√	√	√		√		2515	601	189
FETA + OLIVE EGGS		√	√	√				401	96	218
15-MINUTE HUNGER-BUSTING PRAWN ZOODLES	√	√		√			√	2560	612	178
FIGALICIOUS TOAST				√	√			2749	350	226
FIRE STARTER TOAST	√		√	√	√	√		1293	309	226
FIVE-MINUTE SATISFIER, THE	√	√	√	√	√	√		1598	382	128
FOR THE LOVE OF LABNEH TOAST						√		1129	270	226
FRESH GREEK HUMMUS	√	√	√	√	√	√		663	158	233
FRESH PRAWN AND PAPAYA SALAD	√	√	√	√			√	1661	397	142
FRIED EGGS 'N' SPICE SWEET POTATO TOAST	√	√	√	√		√	√	506	121	201
GET FIGGY WITH IT FLATBREAD			√	√				1678	401	236
GIMME A LITTLE ZING BOWL		√	√			√		1644	393	58
GREEN EGGS TOAST	√		√	√		√		711	170	226
GREEN SUPREME LAYERED SMOOTHIE	√	√			√	√	√	1526	364	77
GUILT-FREE STICKY DATE SMOOTHIE	√	√		√	√	√	√	1477	353	107
HEAT OF THE NIGHT CHICKEN BOWL	√		√					2109	504	181
HARISSA EGGS	√	√	√	√	√	√	√	684	163	218
HARISSA HUMMUS		√	√	√		√		684	163	232
HOLY GUACAMOLE TOAST			√	√		√		1058	253	226
HOT CHOCOLATE		√	√	√	√	√	√	1201	287	69
HOT HARISSA SAVOURY YOGHURT		√	√	√		√		920	220	194
ISLAND DREAMING SMOOTHIE BOWL	√	√	√	√	√	√	√	1201	287	104
IT'S ALL POKE BOWL	√		√	√				2117	506	171
IT TAKES TWO TO MANGO WHIPPED SMOOTHIE	√	√	√	√	√	√	√	1284	307	66
KALE AND MUSHROOM RICE BOWL	√		√	√				2017	482	186
KIMCHI EGGS	√	√	√	√		√	√	284	68	218
LABNEH LOVE SOCCA FLATBREAD		√	√	√		√		665	159	211

RECIPE	DF	GF	NF	SF	V	VG	P	Kj	Cal	Page
LAYER CAKE SMOOTHIE		√		√		√		1242	297	96
LEMON PROTEIN BALLS	√	√			√	√	√	694	166	199
LENTIL AS ANYTHING SALAD	√	√	√	√		√		1820	435	137
MAPLE MISO PUMPKIN WITH SOBA NOODLE	√		√	√	√	√		1858	444	124
MAPLE SPROUT AND KALE SALAD	√	√		√	√	√	√	912	218	146
MISS SAIGON BRUSSELS SPROUTS BOWL	√	√	√	√			√	1310	313	163
MORNING FUEL	√	√		√	√	√	√	1389	332	111
MYKONOS SUMMER NIGHT'S SALAD	√	√	√	√		√		1351	323	138
NEAPOLITAN LAYERED SMOOTHIE	√	√		√	√	√	√	1410	337	70
NO BETTER THAN FETA AVOCADO		√	√	√		√		1129	270	207
NOURISHING ROAST VEGGIE BOWL	√		√	√	√	√	√	2272	543	167
OLIVE YOU SWEET POTATO TOAST	√	√	√	√	√	√		3	125	201
PBH SOCCA FLATBREAD	√	√				√		1381	330	211
PBM SWEET POTATO TOAST	√	√			√	√		791	189	201
PESTO EGGS		√		√		√		397	95	218
PESTO HUMMUS		√		√		√		711	170	233
PINE-ING FOR YOU	√	√	√	√	√	√	√	1251	299	112
PINE NUTS + PARSLEY HUMMUS	√	√		√	√	√		692	165	232
POMEGRANATE FLUSH	√		√	√	√	√	√	1263	302	112
POMEGRANATE HUMMUS	√	√	√	√	√	√		581	139	233
POMEGRANATE POP AVOCADO		√	√	√		√		1033	247	207
PRETTY IN PINK		√	√	√		√		1619	387	84
PROSCUITTO EGGS	√	√	√	√			√	489	117	218
PUMPKIN AND MACADAMIA CROWD PLEASER	√	√		√	√	√	√	2498	597	131
PURE CURE, THE		√				√		1418	339	83
PURIST, THE	√	√	√	√	√	√	√	607	145	87
QUICK AND EASY FROZEN YOGHURT BERRIES	√		√			√		456	109	240
QUINOA BREKKIE BOWL	√	√	√	√	√	√	√	1573	376	160
RADISH EGGS	√	√	√	√	√	√	√	276	66	218
RAD-O-CADO HUMMUS	√	√	√	√	√	√		922	220	233
RASPBERRY COCONUT BALLS	√		√	√	√	√	√	368	88	235
RAW BOUNTYFUL SLICE	√	√	√		√	√		1276	305	221
RED PEPPER EGGS	√	√	√	√	√	√	√	305	73	218
RESTORE SMOOTHIE			√	√		√		995	238	61
ROASTED RED PEPPER HUMMUS	√	√	√	√	√	√		830	198	232

RECIPE	DF	GF	NF	SF	V	VG	P	Kj	Cal	Page
SALTED CARAMEL DELIGHTS		√		√		√		535	128	229
SANTORINI SALMON BOWL		√	√	√			√	1824	436	164
SAY CHEESE SWEET POTATO TOAST		√	√	√		√		661	158	201
SESAME CHICKEN WITH ASIAN CABBAGE SLAW	√		√					2159	516	174
SKIN DEEP	√	√		√	√	√	√	954	228	95
SKINNY AND SWIISH WHIPPED SUPERFOOD BOWL	√	√	√	√	√	√	√	443	106	103
SKINNY DETOX	√	√	√	√	√	√	√	920	220	95
SKINNY PASSION POWER SMOOTHIE	√	√	√	√	√	√	√	912	218	73
SMASHED PEAS SWEET POTATO TOAST		√	√	√		√		899	215	201
SMOKED SALMON SWEET POTATO TOAST	√	√	√	√	√	√		740	177	201
SMOKED TROUT AND MANGO SALAD	√	√	√	√			√	1356	324	123
SMOKED TROUT EGGS	√	√	√	√			√	456	109	218
SMOKY AVO EGGS	√	√	√	√	√	√	√	498	119	218
SOUNDS FISHY AVOCADO	√	√	√	√			√	933	223	207
SPANISH CORN EGGS	√	√	√	√	√	√	√	339	81	218
SPICE UP MY LIFE AVOCADO	√	√	√	√	√	√	√	418	100	207
STICKY ONION EGGS	√	√	√	√	√	√	√	464	111	218
STRAWBERRY FIELDS FROZEN YOGHURT BERRIES		√	√			√		498	118	240
SUPERFOOD ENERGY BALLS	√	√			√	√		636	1	230
SUPER GREEN SUPERFOOD POPS	√	√	√	√	√	√	√	226	54	243
SUPER POWER SALAD	√	√	√	√		√	√	1816	434	150
SWEET DREAMS SMOOTHIE	√			√	√	√	√	1121	268	74
SWEET POTATO NOODLES		√		√		√		1954	467	168
TOTALLY SUBLIME VERMICELLI SALAD	√		√		√	√	√	1351	323	141
TURMERIC AND GINGER BREW	√	√	√	√	√	√	√	79	19	49
TURN UP THE BEET	√	√	√	√	√	√	√	853	204	111
TWO-MINUTE STRAWBERRY GELATO	√	√	√	√	√	√	√	201	48	208
ULTIMATE FIGHTER	√	√	√	√	√	√	√	749	179	108
WHIP IT AND DIP IT		√	√	√		√		1983	474	215
YOU, ME AND CAPRI SALAD		√	√	√			√	1770	423	149
YOU'RE RADISHING AVOCADO		√	√	√		√		1050	251	207
YOU'VE GOT KALE	√	√	√			√	√	816	195	83
ZA'ATAR HUMMUS	√	√		√	√	√		705	168	233
ZA'ATAR SWEET POTATO TOAST	√	√	√	√	√	√	√	954	228	201
ZESTY ZA'ATAR SAVOURY YOGHURT		√	√	√		√		866	207	195

INDEX

THANK YOU

To our incredible readers and our SWIISH.com community: we couldn't be more humbled and grateful on a daily basis by how much you love and support all we do. Thank you for sharing in our daily lives and being part of our story from the beginning. We love that we are all in this together. We've said it before, but we'll say it again: nothing makes us happier than being part of your health and wellbeing journeys, and knowing that you love our recipes. This is for you.

To our families: without you, we couldn't do any of the things we love and are so passionate about. Your love and support are deeply treasured and your patience (particularly when we're on deadline!) is so appreciated. We love you all so much. Thank you for all that you do for us. Mum, Dad, Manfred and Margitta: you're the best and we love you. Margitta, we miss you and know you're watching over us. From Sal, to Marcus and Annabelle and Elyssa: you are the loves of my life. Thank you for believing in me; I couldn't love you more if I tried.

To our SWIISH.com team: we love you all so much and appreciate all that you do. We love having you as part of our extended family and sharing in the vision for our readers and community.

To Claire Kingston, Sarah Baker, David Dalton, Peter Brew-Bevan, Ben Dearnley, Daniella Haggar, Sarah Odgers, Ross Dobson, Michelle Noerianto and everyone else who worked with us on this book: thank you for your continued passion, commitment and belief in us. It's wonderful to work with you all. We are so appreciative.

For the lifestyle images throughout the book, thanks to Peter Brew-Bevan (pages 8, 20, 29, 255 top right and 256) and to Daniella Haggar (pages 5, 13, 17, 24–5, 30, 35, 38, 42–3, 48, 80–1, 93, 100 top, 101 middle left, 134–5, 172–3, 216–17, 244–5, 254 and 255 top left, middle, bottom left and bottom right). Thanks also to Alex Barron at Watson's Bay Boutique Hotel, Sydney, for hosting us in the Top Deck area (pages 5, 30, 35, 93, 100 top, 101 middle left, 134–5, 172–3, and 255 middle and bottom left).

BEHIND THE GREEN SCENES

CONNECT WITH US

We'd love for you to check in with us at SWIISH.com, and subscribe for new recipes, videos, tips, tricks, giveaways and lots more.

You can also find us:
* On **Instagram** at @swiishbysallyo
* On **Twitter** at twitter.com/swiishbysallyo
* On **Facebook** at facebook.com/swiishbysallyobermeder

Don't forget to tag SWIISH in your snaps, selfies, healthies (healthy selfies!) and share with us your favourite recipes.

Connect with **Sally Obermeder**:
* On **Instagram** at @sallyobermeder
* On **Twitter** at twitter.com/sallyobermeder
* On **Facebook** at facebook.com/sallyobermeder

Connect with **Maha Koraiem**:
* On **Instagram** at @maha_koraiem
* On **Twitter** at twitter.com/maha_koraiem
* On **Facebook** at facebook.com/maha.koraiem